Pragmatic Python Programming

Learning Python the Smart Way

Gabor Guta

Apress®

Pragmatic Python Programming: Learning Python the Smart Way

Gabor Guta
Budapest, Hungary

ISBN-13 (pbk): 978-1-4842-8151-2   ISBN-13 (electronic): 978-1-4842-8152-9
https://doi.org/10.1007/978-1-4842-8152-9

Managing Director, Apress Media LLC: Welmoed Spahr
Acquisitions Editor: Celestin Suresh John
Development Editor: James Markham
Coordinating Editor: Mark Powers
Copyeditor: Kim Wimpsett

Cover designed by eStudioCalamar

Cover image by David Clode on Unsplash (www.unsplash.com)

Distributed to the book trade worldwide by Apress Media, LLC, 1 New York Plaza, New York, NY 10004, U.S.A. Phone 1-800-SPRINGER, fax (201) 348-4505, e-mail orders-ny@springer-sbm. com, or visit www.springeronline.com. Apress Media, LLC is a California LLC and the sole member (owner) is Springer Science + Business Media Finance Inc (SSBM Finance Inc). SSBM Finance Inc is a **Delaware** corporation.

For information on translations, please e-mail booktranslations@springernature.com; for reprint, paperback, or audio rights, please e-mail bookpermissions@springernature.com.

Apress titles may be purchased in bulk for academic, corporate, or promotional use. eBook versions and licenses are also available for most titles. For more information, reference our Print and eBook Bulk Sales web page at www.apress.com/bulk-sales.

Any source code or other supplementary material referenced by the author in this book is available to readers on GitHub (https://github.com/Apress/pragmatic-python-programming). For more detailed information, please visit www.apress.com/source-code.

Printed on acid-free paper

I am thankful to my wife and to my family for their endurance and support.

Table of Contents

About the Author

 **Gabor Guta** studied and carried out research at the Research Institute for Symbolic Computation, Johannes Kepler University, Linz, to gain an understanding of the formal meaning of programming languages. He worked on complex technology transfer, cheminformatics, and bioinformatics projects where both strong theoretical background and practical software development skills were crucial. Currently, he is developing distributed software for an open data project. Besides his software development work, he has been continuously training people both in academic and industrial settings. He has been actively teaching Python since 2017.

About the Technical Reviewer

 **Joshua Willman** began using Python in 2015 when he needed to build neural networks using machine learning libraries for image classification. While building large image datasets for his research, he needed to build a program that would simplify the workload and labeling process, which introduced him to PyQt. Since then, he has tried to dive into everything that is Python.

He currently works as a Python developer, building projects to help others learn more about coding in Python for game development, AI, and machine learning. Recently, he set up the site redhuli.io to explore his and others' interests in utilizing programming for creativity.

He is the author of *Modern PyQt: Create GUI Applications for Project Management, Computer Vision, and Data Analysis* and *Beginning PyQt: A Hands-on Approach to GUI Programming*, both published by Apress.

Acknowledgments

I am thankful to István Juhász, my former diploma supervisor; without his encouragement and enthusiastic support, this book could not have come into existence. I am grateful to my friend László Szathmáry, who helped me as an experienced Python developer and trainer with his insightful feedback.

Introduction

Communication gaps can build up in IT workplaces between developers and other roles not requiring programming skills. This gap frequently hurts the project's progress and makes cooperation between participants difficult. My intention is to bridge this gap with this book by explaining the common mental models with which humans think. I will also demonstrate the way these models are applied during the programming process.
The book is based on more than two decades of training and software development experience. Python is not only a popular and modern programming language, but it is also an easy-to-learn and efficient tool to reach your goals.

I will not provide too many hands-on exercises and technical details (how an operating system is built, the way a networking protocol works, etc.). Regrettably, I cannot offer a quick option to acquire these skills, as the only way to achieve these skills is with extensive amounts of practice and troubleshooting. This book will give you a strong basis for starting that practice.

Structure and Use of the Book

My intention with the book is to discuss the Python language, along the key concepts, using a new approach. Every chapter of the book starts with the introduction of a particular concept and then goes through the advanced features of the language (as if it were a reference manual).

- For those who are just getting acquainted with the language and whose aim is only to understand the major concepts of the programming language, focusing on the first parts of the chapters is recommended. Please feel free to skip the "Advanced Features" sections. Studying Appendix A will also be worthwhile.

- For those who are just becoming acquainted with the language aiming to learn how to program, I recommend running and experimenting with the examples. It will be worthwhile to skim the "Advanced Features" section and then return to that section later for a detailed reading.

- For experienced software developers, it is worthwhile to quickly read the first parts of each chapter by paying attention to the concepts in the Python language that do not exist in other program languages. For such readers, the "Advanced Features" sections at the end of the chapters are mandatory.

Figures use the UML notation, and a short description of their meaning is shown at the end of Chapters 1, 3, 4, and 5. In the source code examples, I deviate sometimes from the Python coding standard due to the page layout constraints. These appear mostly with short or shortened names and 40- to 50-character lines. Program code examples are conceptually independent units, but they assume former examples of the book have been run, since they may refer to definitions in them. The examples are based on the most up-to-date Python 3.10.2 version available when writing the book. Most of the examples can be run in versions 3.8.x and 3.9.x, which are the most widespread at this time. Results of the examples are intentionally not published in the book. The source code in the book is available for download and you can experiment with it.

Source Code

All source code used in this book is available for you to download from `https://github.com/Apress/pragmatic-python-programming`.

Installing an Environment

The installation steps for the most widespread operating systems (Windows 10, macOS, Ubuntu Linux 22.04 LTS) are described here so you can run the examples in this book. For another operating system, you can find assistance on the Internet.

Installation on Windows 10

Follow these steps to install and run Python on Windows 10:

1. Open `http://python.org` in a browser, select the Downloads menu, and then select Python 3.10.2 (or a newer version if it's offered).

2. The browser automatically launches the download or displays the file download dialog, which starts the download.

3. After selecting the Download menu, the newly downloaded file appears: `python-3.10.2.exe`. Launch the installer by clicking the filename.

4. Select the Add Python 3.10 to PATH option in the installation window and click the "Install now" button.

5. The installer continues to inform you about the status of installation. At the end of the installation, select the "Disable path length limit" option and click the Close button.

6. Click the magnifying glass icon next to the Windows icon, and start typing in **cmd**. The icon for the command line appears; open it by pressing Enter.

7. Install and start a Jupyter lab by entering the `python -m pip install jupyterlab` and `jupyter lab` commands (assuming that the working directory will be the user directory).

8. After launching the Jupyter lab, the contents of the working directory will be displayed. If you download the examples, selecting a file will open it. Or click the New button and select the Python 3 option; an empty notebook will open in a new browser window.

9. Your Jupyter notebook is built up from cells. The content of the cells can be program code, text, or something else. The default content of the cells is the Python program code you type in. A cell can be run by pressing Shift+Enter. The value of the latest expression will appear under the cell.

Installation on macOS

Follow these steps to install and run Python on macOS:

1. Open http://python.org in a browser and select the Downloads menu. Then select Python 3.10.2 (or a newer version if it's offered).

2. The browser automatically launches the download or displays the file download dialog, which starts the download.

3. After selecting the Download menu, the newly downloaded file appears: python-3.10.2-macosx10.9.pkg. Launch the installer by clicking this name.

4. Confirm the default settings by clicking the Continue buttons in consecutive windows in the browser and then selecting the Install button to launch the installation.

5. The installer continues to inform you about the status of installation. At the end of the installation, click the Close button.

6. Select the Launchpad and start to type in the term word. The icon for the Terminal appears; click the icon to open the Terminal.

7. Install and start a Jupyter lab by entering the python -m pip install jupyterlab and jupyter lab commands (assuming that the working directory will be the user directory).

8. After launching the Jupyter lab, the contents of the working directory will be displayed. If you downloaded the examples earlier, selecting the directory will open it. If you click the New button and select the Python 3 option, an empty notebook will open in a new browser window.

9. Your Jupyter notebook is built up from cells. The content of the cells can be program code, text, or something else. The default content of the cells is the Python program code you type in. A cell can be run by pressing Shift+Enter. The value of the latest expression will appear under the cell.

Installation on Ubuntu Linux 22.04

Python 3.10.x version is installed by default. Follow these steps to run Python on Ubuntu Linux 22.04:

1. Press the Windows key, and start to type in the word `term`. The icon of the terminal appears; open it by clicking the icon.

2. Install and start a Jupyter lab by entering the `python -m pip install jupyterlab` and `jupyter lab` commands (by assuming that the working directory will be the user directory).

3. After launching the Jupyter lab, the contents of the working directory will be displayed. If the examples were downloaded earlier, you can open them by selecting it. If you click the New button and select the Python 3 option, an empty notebook will open in a new browser window.

4. Your Jupyter notebook is built up from cells. The content of the cells can be program code, text, or something else. The default content of cells is the Python program code you type in. A cell can be run by pressing Shift+Enter. The value of the latest expression will appear under the cell.

After installing a Jupyter lab, you can download the accompanying Jupyter notebook to its working directory. Now, you are ready to start your journey in the world of the Python programming language.

CHAPTER 1

Expression: How to Compute

"Expressions are formed from operators and operands."

Brian W. Kernighan, Dennis M. Ritchie

One of the basic building blocks of programming languages is the *expression*, which serves to describe a logical or mathematical relation. In this chapter, you will learn how exactly an expression denotes relations between objects, how expressions can be used in statements, and how the objects can be labeled by names.

As an example, take the calculation of the price of an order. The formula is as follows: the price of the product multiplied by the quantity plus the shipping cost. Let's look at how it is calculated in Python if the product's price is 500 USD, two pieces are ordered, and the shipping cost is 200 USD.

Listing 1-1 shows an expression consisting of numbers (integers) and operators. The order of operations is determined by specific rules (much like those you can recall from your elementary school education).

Listing 1-1. A Simple Expression

```
500*2 + 200
```

© Gabor Guta 2022

G. Guta, *Pragmatic Python Programming*, https://doi.org/10.1007/978-1-4842-8152-9_1

Caution   Spaces should not be inserted before the expressions and statements shown in this chapter, and they should not be broken into multiple lines. This is important as the space(s), tabulators at the beginning of the lines, and line breaks do have a special meaning in Python. The relevant rules are detailed later in the chapter.

The computer processes the expression in Listing 1-1 in multiple steps. Integers are considered objects, which, in this case, are integer type ones. The structure referred to as the *expression tree* and shown in Figure 1-1a is constructed of integer objects and operators. In the figure the rectangles are objects or operators; if the objects correspond to an operator, they are linked with lines to the operator. You can find a bit more about this standard notion at the end of the chapter. The expression tree is constructed by assigning objects to an operator, among which the operation is to be performed. In the expression tree, the result of another operator can also be assigned to an operator, not just an object. This is indicated by connecting it to another operator, meaning that it is to be performed first, and the resulting object will be used then. The uppermost element of the expression tree is the operator to be performed last.

The computer interprets the expression tree by performing the operators between objects first. In the example, this is the leftmost multiplicative operator at the bottom. The result of this operator will be a new integer object with the value of 1000. Figure 1-1b shows the resulting intermediate expression tree, along with the addition operator between the integer objects with the values 1000 and 200, and the result is an integer object value 1200, as shown in Figure 1-1c.

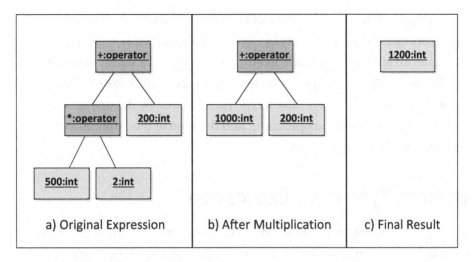

Figures 1-1a, 1-1b, and 1-1c. *Simple expression*

If there is uncertainty about the operation order, placing brackets is encouraged, as in Listing 1-2.

Listing 1-2. Fully Parenthesized Expression

```
((500*2) + 200)
```

The expression without brackets and the fully bracketed expression have the same meaning for the computer. Notably, the expressions can be of any complexity; however, there is a certain level of complexity where they become difficult to understand.

Expressions with Additional Types

In Listing 1-1, we have seen integers as objects on which to perform the operators. Expressions, however, can be used in the general sense, whereas operators can be performed between objects of various types. In addition to the integer type objects, other types of objects will also be covered, e.g., Boolean types (true/false values) and strings. You will learn how to create your own type in Chapter 3.

The type of the particular object is important also because certain operators can be executed only by objects of a specified type. If, for example, an attempt was made to add an integer and a string, an error will be raised. When the operation has been successfully executed, the resulting object will always have a type (determined by the operation, the object performing the operation, and the type of the other object participating in the operation).

Boolean Type in an Expression

Listing 1-3 shows an expression where two integers are compared. When comparing two integers, the created new value will be of the Boolean type. The true value is denoted by the word True, while the false value is represented by False. Part of this expression tree on the left side of the comparison sign is the same as the previous example, and its evaluation is also the same. Thus, the last step will be carrying out the comparison, wherein the result of comparing the two integers will be a True object.

Listing 1-3. Boolean Expression

```
500*2 + 200 >= 1000
```

String Type in an Expression

Listing 1-4 contains string objects. The string type objects are characters between single or double quotation marks. From these quotation marks, the computer will know where characters forming the string begin and where they end and that there is no need to interpret them, just to handle them as any text. The addition operator between strings means concatenation. The first step upon evaluation of this expression is the formation of a novel string object from the two left string objects, and then in the next step, the resulting string object is created by the concatenation of the newly created string object and the right-side object.

Listing 1-4. Operation Between Strings

```
'no' + ' ' + 'discount'
```

Expressions with Conditional Operators

A conditional expression can describe the computation that the result should be one or another value depending on some condition. This expression is interpreted among three objects. The first object is of any type, the supposed value when the condition is fulfilled. The second object is of Boolean type, the condition itself, after the word `if`. The last object is the expected value when the condition is not fulfilled, located after the word `else`. (As you would expect, any of the objects can be substituted with an expression.) Listing 1-5 demonstrates how to combine the conditional expression with the types reviewed so far.

Listing 1-5. Conditional Expression

```
'5%' if 500*2+200 >= 1000 else 'none'
```

The task solved by the example is the following: if the amount of the order is greater than 1000, a string containing the discount rate would be created with the values 5% or none. Figure 1-2 shows the expression trees formed upon evaluation of the expression.

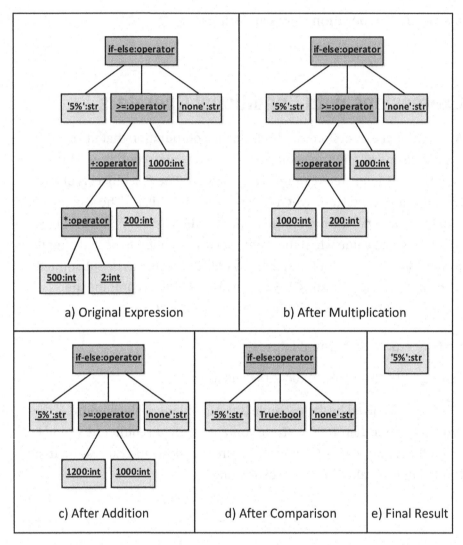

Figures 1-2a, 1-2b, 1-2c, 1-2d, and 1-2e. *Expression with multiple types*

Floating-Point Number Type in an Expression

Finally, let's look at the number types. Three kinds of number types are distinguished in Python: integers, floating, and complex numbers. You have already seen examples for the integers. The float type can store the decimal fractions. Listing 1-6 shows an expression wherein two decimal fractions with the same value are added (the first number object was written in the usual format as 0.05, while the other one was in $5*10^{-2}$ format).

Listing 1-6. Floating-Point Numbers

```
0.05 == 5e-2
```

Complex Number Type in an Expression

Complex numbers (used in higher mathematical computations) are called the *complex type*. The simplest way a complex number could be considered is a pair of decimal fractions wherein the first one is the real value, and the second one is the imaginary one. The imaginary value corresponds to the square root of -1. It is checked in Listing 1-7, if $(0+1j)^2$ is really equal to the value of -1.

Listing 1-7. Complex Numbers

```
(0+1j)**2 == -1
```

During the design of the Python language, it was a vital design decision that it should contain a small number of built-in types, and at first sight, the behavior of those types is the same as that of the other, not built-in types. Only five data types are examined more thoroughly here; the rest will be discussed in Chapters 5 and 6.

Tip   In the Python language, it is possible to put the comparisons into a chain, meaning the 0 < a and a < 100 expressions can be written in the form of 0 < a < 100. The two expressions are equivalent, except that in the second case the expression standing in the place of a is computed only once. This notation can also be used between more than two comparisons.

Variable Names

Now that we have seen how to carry out computation in specific cases, let's look at how a computation can be generalized. For this case, objects are assigned to variable names. Variable names may be thought of most simply as labels. Variable names usually begin with a letter and continue with letters or digits. The expression in Listing 1-5 could be rewritten by first assigning the numbers to variable names, as shown in Listing 1-8. The advantage of this approach is that in case we were to compute the expression for other numbers, we simply change only the assignment statements in lines 1–3 and would not have to modify the expressions.

Listing 1-8. Assignment Statements

```
PRICE = 500
QUANTITY = 2
LIMIT = 1000
total_amount = PRICE * QUANTITY
d_available = total_amount >= LIMIT
discount = '5%' if d_available else 'none'
```

To express the intent that the variable names to which the value once assigned will not require change, the variable names are capitalized. This notation is not more than a convention, and the Python language does not prevent them from being changed.

The resulting expression is thus much easier to understand. Importantly, not the formula itself is assigned to the variable name, but an object created upon computation of the expression instead. It is always necessary to assign an object to the variable name before it is used (it must appear on the left side of the equation before it can appear on the right side).

Variable names are also used to break down complicated expressions into simpler ones. This can be accomplished by assigning some part of the expression to the variable names and then using the variable names in place of the extracted expressions. Furthermore, if the variable names assigned to the particular expressions are chosen well, the meaning of the expression will be more explicit.

Tip   When do you have to insert space between characters? The short answer is: when the characters without space would evidently have a different meaning. For example, the meanings of a + b and a+b are the same; thus, the space can be left out. But the cases of a b and ab are different; the two names (identifiers) would become a single name. Table 1-1 shows some examples. If spaces do not affect the meaning, they can be inserted or omitted, depending on readability. The detailed answer will be given in the section "Advanced Details."

Table 1-1. *Effects of Spaces Between Characters*

Without Space	With Space	Interpretation
a+b	a + b	Identical.
a=2	a = 2	Identical.
ab	a b	Adding a space between alphabetic characters turns the single name into two separate names, which are in most cases syntactically incorrect (an important exception is when one of the names is a keyword).
12	1 2	Adding a space between numeric characters turns a single literal into two separate literals, which are in most cases syntactically incorrect.

(continued)

9

Table 1-1. (*continued*)

Without Space	With Space	Interpretation
a1	a 1	Adding a space between an alphabetic and a numeric characters turns the single name into a name and a literal, which are in most cases syntactically incorrect (an important exception is when the name is a keyword).
1a	1 a	Adding a space between a numeric and an alphabetic characters turns the syntactically incorrect character sequence into a literal and a name, which are in most cases also syntactically incorrect (an important exception is when the name is a keyword like 1 or); in earlier versions of Python 1or character sequence was syntactically correct, but know it is deprecated and will cause a syntax error in the future.

Statements

Listing 1-8 showed a program consisting of multiple lines. Each line is one statement, more precisely an assignment statement. Programs consist of statements that are executed one after the other, thereby exerting some effect on their environment. The default in Python is that one line is one statement. The recommended maximal line length is 79 characters. Listing 1-9 shows how a long statement can be stretched to multiple lines (lines 3 to 7) or multiple statements can be condensed into a single line (line 7). When a line is too short for a statement, part of the statement can be brought over to the following line after an end-of-line backslash (\). Should we want to compact multiple statements in a line, the statements would have to be separated by a semicolon (;). Both notations should generally be avoided.

Listing 1-9. Statements

```
PRICE = 500
QUANTITY = 2
PRICE = \
500
QUANTITY = \
2
PRICE = 500; QUANTITY = 2
```

Integer objects are assigned to variable names in the previous example. If, for example, statements in the second and third lines were replaced, an error would occur since there are no objects yet assigned to the quantity label. It is also a consequence of the stepwise statement execution that no object assigned to a variable name would change (except for the unit price) if one more PRICE = 450 line were inserted at the end of the program. For example, the d_available variable name would still point to an object with a true value. To change the assignments, the statements from line 3 to line 5 would have to be re-executed.

The assignment statement consists of a name, an assignment operator, and an expression. In Python, the equal sign means the result of the right-side expression is assigned to the left-side variable name. (The double equal sign is used to test the equality of two expressions.) The assignment statement is not an expression; therefore, it does not have a return value. To obtain an object assigned to the variable name as an expression, the := walrus operator can be used, but it can be used only in restricted cases (details of the walrus operator will be explained in Chapter 5).

Deletion of a Variable Name

Variable names can also be deleted by the del statement. In Listing 1-10, after the variable name difference is deleted, reading the variable name content results in an error. Objects assigned to the variable names are automatically unallocated when they are not referenced anymore (i.e., when they are not assigned to any variable names). Referencing to the variable name difference after Listing 1-10 would cause a NameError error.

Listing 1-10. Deletion of a Variable Name

```
difference = 550 - 500
del difference
```

Note   The source code elements are the expressions, statements, and concepts touched upon later. The name source code (a code readable for humans) originates from the fact that it is the source of the executable code run by the computer. Files containing the source code are referred to as *source files*. We can speak about a program when we want to emphasize that it is about the source code realizing an independent and meaningful task. For completeness, programs that can be run as direct source code are usually called *scripts*. Unfortunately, these denominations are often used loosely in the literature and leave the correct interpretation to the reader.

Additional Language Constructs

In the program fragments described so far, objects are expressed by specific integer, string, and Boolean (True and False) values. Their collective term is *literals*. Operators are used between them. You have seen the if and else names in the conditional expressions. Names with such special meaning are called *keywords*. The pass keyword represents the no operation statement. This statement is used to designate that a statement would follow, but our deliberate intention is that nothing happens at that point of the program.

The text located after the character # up to the end of the line is called a *comment* that is used to place any textual information. A comment is a message to the reader of the source code and can help in understanding the program. If variable names in the program are chosen well, a minimum amount of commenting is necessary.

Multiline comments can be achieved with multiline strings. Multiline strings start and end with a triple quotation mark (typically """), and line breaks are allowed inside the string. Technically these are not comments, but expressions. So, multiline comments must always start in a separate new line. You will see in Chapter 2 that these multiline comments can have a special role depending on their position in the source code. Listing 1-11 shows some examples.

Listing 1-11. Pass Statement and Comments

```
pass #this statement does nothing
# this line is only a comment
""" these lines form
a multiline
comment """
```

Statements and Expressions in Practice

With type annotations, the expected type of object to be assigned to the variable name can be expressed. Python is a dynamically typed language, which means that the type of a variable name depends solely on the type of the assigned object. This means that currently Python does not check if these type annotations are correct. Originally, Python did not have any notation to explicitly add typing information as it was considered extra effort to maintain and makes the code more inflexible. As Python is used for large and complex programs, these annotations become more useful for the developers and tools. External tools can be used to verify whether the assigned object types are consistent with the type annotations without running the program. Use of external tools will be described in Chapter 6. The type is specified after the variable name, separated from it by a colon, as shown in the Listing 1-12.

Listing 1-12. Assignments with Type Definitions

```
PRICE: int = 500
QUANTITY: int = 2
LIMIT: int = 1000
total_amount: int = PRICE * QUANTITY
d_available: bool = total amount >= LIMIT
discount: str = '5%' if d_available else 'none'
```

It is crucial for the readability of the program to put spaces in certain spots in the expressions and statements. The documentation of Python contains a recommendation for the placement of spaces to ensure the best readability:

- It is recommended to insert a space on both sides of an equal signs; and put a space only after colons.

- Extra spaces should not be inserted for parentheses, but spaces are recommended so that the context is preserved.

- Spaces are inserted around the operators as a default;
  an exception is if the order of operations in the
  expression is other than simply from left to right, since
  there are parentheses, or certain operations should
  be executed sooner. In this case, spaces are removed
  around operations executed sooner, such as in the case
  of (a+2) * (b+4) or a*2 + b*4.

If required, the aim or use of the statements can be documented by a comment placed after it (beginning with the character #, as discussed earlier). Lengthier comments can be placed among the statement lines, and each line should begin with the character #. It is recommended that the information recorded here should be such that it could not be figured out from the variable names and the type annotations.

Tip   An expression can be included in the so-called formatted string literals (or *f-strings*). In this case, there is a letter *f* (as shown in Listing 1-13) before the string's opening quotation mark, and the expressions are within the quotation marks, between the braces. The result of these expressions will be inserted after they are converted to a string.

In the f-strings, format specifiers can also be added after the expression, separated by a colon (:). Listing 1-14 shows the format of the variable PRICE1 as a decimal fraction with two decimal places and shows writing out variable PRICE2 as an integer filled with 0s, up to five digits.

Listing 1-13. Formatted String Literals

```
PRICE1 = 10
PRICE2 = 2500
Difference of f'{PRICE1} and {PRICE2} is {PRICE2-PRICE1}'
```

Listing 1-14. Formatted String Literals with Format Specifiers

```
f'{PRICE1:.2f}, {PRICE2:05d}'
```

Advanced Details

This section describes technical details in reference manual style and advanced concepts that may need more technical background.

Names

You saw that names (also called *identifiers*) can be given to objects. The following characters can be present in a name: beginning with a letter or an underscore and continuing with a letter-like character, underscore, or digit. Letter-like means that other categories are added to characters considered letters in the Unicode standard, namely, the "nonspacing mark," the "spacing combining mark," and the "connector punctuation" categories. Within names Python discriminates lowercase and uppercase letters, but certain character combinations can be regarded the same according to the NFKC standard. It is recommended to use only letters of the English alphabet in names.

Keywords and Special Names

There are certain names that have special meaning in Python; these are called *keywords* and are shown in Table 1-2. You have already learned the meanings of the keywords True and False, and the meanings of the other ones will be gradually introduced in subsequent chapters.

Table 1-2. *Keywords*

and	as	assert	async	await
break	class	continue	def	del
elif	else	except	False	finally
for	from	global	if	import
in	is	lambda	None	nonlocal
not	or	pass	raise	return
True	try	while	with	yield

Names both beginning and ending with a double underscore character may have a special meaning in the Python language. Therefore, your own variables should not be denoted in this way. A single or double underscore only at the beginning of the name is not subject to this restriction. Their function is detailed in Chapter 3. A single underscore after a variable name is used in case the name would otherwise be a keyword. Finally, a single underscore character as a variable name is used to signal that the value of the variable won't be used, but defining a variable name is required for syntactic constraints.

Literals

Literals represent objects corresponding to their meanings. Rules applied to the bool, complex, float, int, and str type values are as follows:

- The value of a Boolean can be true or false. The true value is denominated by True, while false is signified by False.

- There are also rules applied for integers. Simple decimal integers begin with a digit that is not zero and continue with any digit. If a zero is written, any integer of zeros can follow, but no other digits. If an integer is written in a system other than decimal, the b, o, or x letters after a zero digit annotate the following number in the binary, octal, or hexadecimal number system; then the particular number itself is written according to the rules of the particular number system. (For example, in terms of the binary number system, digits can be only 0 or 1, while in the case of the hexadecimal system, besides the number 9, the lowercase or uppercase letters between *A* and *F* are allowed. Lowercase or uppercase letters are both allowed for the letters denoting the number system, as they are for the numbers in the hexadecimal system.) Numbers can always be separated by underscoring. Listing 1-15 shows examples of the previously mentioned syntax.

Listing 1-15. Integers in Various Number Systems

```
42
0b10_1010
0o52
0x2A
```

- Floats or, more precisely, floating-point numbers, are those always represented in the decimal system: a dot is placed within the integer or around it, or the integer exponent of number 10 multiplying the particular number is written after the number, separated by a letter e. Floating-point numbers used in Python are according to the IEEE 754 standard.

- Complex numbers, in turn, can be represented by two floats. One of them is the imaginary part that is denoted by a letter j written after a float; according to this notation, the 1j corresponds to the square root of -1.

- Strings are written between pairs of quotation marks, ' or ". The meanings of the two kinds of quotation marks are the same, but it is recommended to select one and use that one consistently. An exception is when the original text itself contains a kind of quotation mark. In this case, it is recommended to use the other kind at both ends of the string. If you want to write a multiline string, it will have to be between the characters of ' ' ' or """. Any character except the quotation mark can appear within a string. If you would like to write the same characters as the opening and closing quotation marks, we have to use a backslash character before them. After the backslash, other characters can denote otherwise not representable characters (according to Table 1-3).

Table 1-3. *Escape Character Table*

Character	Meaning
\ and "new line"	The backslash and the new line will be ignored.
\\	The backslash itself (\).
\a	ASCII bell character (BEL).
\b	ASCII backspace (BS).
\f	ASCII form feed (FF).
\n	ASCII linefeed (LF).
\r	ASCII carriage return (CR).
\t	ASCII horizontal tabulation (TAB).
\v	ASCII vertical tabulation (VT).
\ooo	Character code with a value of ooo in an octal number system.
\xhh	Character code with a value of hh in a hexadecimal number system.

- The character r can be present before strings with the effect of the backslash character working as a simple character. This is useful in describing access paths (for example, the r 'C:\Users' notation is equivalent to 'C:\\Users') and regular expressions. The letter f can also be present before strings, meaning that if an expression is written between the characters { and }, it is computed, and the result will be inserted as a string (see the former paragraph on formatted string literals). The letter b may also occur; you can find a more detailed description about it in Appendix B.

Characters with Special Meaning

Table 1-4 summarizes characters having a special meaning in Python. Operations are denoted in the expressions by the operator characters. Delimiters occur primarily in statements. Other special characters serve to denote values or comments. There are characters that can be used only in literals.

Table 1-4. *Characters with Special Meaning*

Category	Characters						
Operators	<<	>>	&	^	~	:=	
	<	>	<=	>=	==	!=	
Delimiters	,	:	.	;	@	=	->
	+=	-=	*=	/=	//=	%=	@=
	&=	|=	^=	<<=	>>=	**=	
Other special characters	'	"	#	\			
Can be used only in strings	$	?	'				

The dot can appear within a decimal fraction. Three consecutive dots may be present one after the other, which is called an *ellipsis literal*. This is not used in core Python, only in some extensions (e.g., NumPy).

Table 1-5 shows that the precedence of the operators is shown downward increasing. Stronger operations will be performed first. If strengths were equal, applying the operations takes place from left to right. An exception is exponentiation with a reverse direction of application.

Table 1-5. *Precedence of Operators*

Operators	Meaning
x := y	Assignment expression
x if y else z	Conditional expression
x or y	Logical or
x and y	Logical and
not x	Logical negation
x in y, x not in y, x is y, x is not y, x < y, x <= y, x > y, x >= y, x != y, x == y	Membership tests, identity tests, and comparisons
x | y	Bitwise or
x ^ y	Bitwise exclusive or
x & y	Bitwise and
x << y, x >> y	Bitwise shift
x + y, x - y	Addition, subtraction
x / y, x // y, x % y	Division, integer division, remainder
+x, -x, ~x	Positive, negative, bitwise negation
x**y	Raising to the power
(x)	Expression in parentheses

Python Standards

The Python language is defined in *The Python Language Reference*. The content of the book covers basically this document. In addition, several language-related standards will be described in the *Python Enhancement Proposals*; they are usually referenced as PEP plus a number. An often mentioned PEP document is PEP 8, which contains a recommendation for formatting the Python source code.

Object Diagram Notation

Figures used in the chapter are represented in the object diagram notation of the Unified Modeling Language (UML). These diagrams can represent objects and their connections of a particular moment. Rectangles represent objects in the diagrams. The names of the objects appear as text written into the rectangle. The names of the objects are always written underlined, optionally with its type after it preceded by a colon. Lines between the rectangles denote connections. Objects in the figures are denoted according to their value, and the value is not represented by a separate instance variable.

Key Takeaways

- In the chapter, you learned about the concept of an expression, which is one of the most important building blocks of programming languages. An expression describes operations between objects. Usually, the goal of their usage is to construct a new object needed for the next step of processing (e.g., calculating the sum of the price of products).

- The statements describe a step of a program and make changes in the execution context. The assignment statement, which assigns an object to a name, is a good example of this. An expression can serve as a statement, but statements cannot stand where expressions are expected.

- The variable name is the first tool to organize your program. For example, a complex expression can be broken into several simpler expressions of which results are assigned to variable names and then combined in a final step.

CHAPTER 2

The Function: Programs as a Series of Statements

"It is usual in mathematics—outside of mathematical logic—to use the word function imprecisely and to apply it to forms such as $y^2 + x$. Because we shall later compute with expressions for functions, we need a distinction between functions and forms and a notation for expressing this distinction. This distinction and a notation for describing it, from which we deviate trivially is given by Church."

John McCarthy et al.

The function is the simplest construct able to describe a behavior. Functions can behave similarly as in math: they compute a number from a given number or numbers. Functions in programming languages are of a somewhat more general construction, though: they generate a new object by executing statements from given objects. In this chapter, you will learn how functions work in programming languages and about related concepts such as blocks.

© Gabor Guta 2022
G. Guta, *Pragmatic Python Programming*, https://doi.org/10.1007/978-1-4842-8152-9_2

Calling a Function

Let's start by looking at how to use the built-in functions that already exist in Python. Using a function usually means executing a function call. The result of the function is referred to as the *returned value*. The computer executes the statements assigned to the function name with the specified objects, and the result object will be obtained. This is expressed by placing a pair of parentheses after the function name, in which parameter objects are enumerated optionally. The enumerated objects are called the *arguments* of the functions. Calling the absolute value function visible in Listing 2-1 will result in a number object with a value of 1. This is exactly what you would expect from the |-1| expression.

Listing 2-1. Calculation of an Absolute Value

```
abs(-1)
```

The function call can be combined with expression notations: it can be present anywhere a reference to an object can be written, and so the arguments of the function can become arbitrarily complicated expressions. From among the built-in mathematical functions you saw examples for the absolute value function (abs()). In addition, there also exists the functions of raising to a power (pow()) and rounding (round()). You can see this in Listing 2-2. The result of price calculation of 3499 with tax (which is 10% in the United States, so the original number must be multiplied by 1.1) is 3848.9, which is rounded to an integer (to 3849) in the example.

Listing 2-2. Calculation of a Rounded Value

```
round(3499 * 1.1)
```

Tip   The built-in types of the Python language cannot always accurately store decimals. This is a consequence of the binary representation of decimals in memory. For example, the 3848.9 value shown in the previous example is stored as 3848.90000000000009. How to store best financial data in Python is described in detail in Chapter 6.

Listing 2-3 shows a more complicated expression. What we are calculating is the gross difference of two net prices. First the rounded gross values of the two prices are calculated in the expression; then these are subtracted from each other. It is visible in the example that the function calls can be embedded, and the result of the abs() function call is assigned to a variable name.

Listing 2-3. Calculation of a More Complicated Expression

```
OLD_NET = 5000
NEW_NET = 6500
VAT_RATE = 1.1

difference_gross = abs(round(OLD_NET*1.1) - round(NEW_NET*1.1))
```

Side Effects of Functions

The function concept in the programming languages is more general than that in the mathematical sense, as previously clarified. An important difference is that functions can have side effects. By side effects, we mean it not only calculates a value and that value will be returned, but it also changes something in its environment: changes the value of an object in the environment of a function, displays text to the screen, saves a file, sends an email on the network, etc.

The Python language even allows a function to not have a result object. In this case, its return value will be a None object. This makes sense, usually, when the function completes its task by causing a side effect (e.g., writing a string to display, writing to a file, etc.).

In Listing 2-4 the function writes Hello World to the screen. (This is a typical first example when teaching a program language.)

Listing 2-4. Function with a Side Effect

```
print('Hello World!')
```

Listing 2-5 shows a practical example, where the print() function has two arguments: one is the string containing the message, and the other is the total amount. These arguments will be printed on a single line separated by spaces. In Listing 2-6, you can see the reverse of the print() function, which reads a line instead of printing it. The line is a string closed by a linefeed; hence, the input() function reads characters until the Enter key is pressed. The result of reading a line does not contain the linefeed character. The input() function receives a parameter as well, a string, which is additionally written out before reading the line.

Listing 2-5. Function with Multiple Parameters

```
total_amount = 1000
print('Order total:', total_amount)
```

Listing 2-6. Input and Output Statements

```
product_name = input('Please, enter the name of the product')
print('The name of the product:', product_name)
```

Function Arguments

Arguments have so far been specified to functions by listing them in due order. This method of argument specification is referred to as *positional parameter specification*. However, it is possible to specify an argument not only according to position but also as a keyword argument.

There are two important arguments of the print() function that can be specified as keyword arguments: the sep and end arguments. These arguments can be strings: the first one specifies which separator character should be printed between the printed values, and the second one specifies what is printed at the end of the line. Among the arguments of the function, the positional arguments should always precede the keyword parameters.

The Python language allows positional or keyword arguments to be optional. In other words, the function will assign them a default value if they are not specified. The keyword arguments of print() can be omitted because they have default values. The default value for the sep parameter is a space, and the default value for the end parameter is a new line (linefeed) character. See Listing 2-7.

Listing 2-7. Specification of Keyword Arguments

```
PRODUCT_NAME = 'Cube'
PRICE = 100
print('The product:', PRODUCT_NAME, end=' ')
print('(', PRICE, ' USD)', sep='')
```

The other feature you can observe is that the print() function has any number of positional parameters. We speak of a variable-length parameter list, and at the function call you specify them as normal fixed parameters. This is useful in cases when it is not known in advance how many arguments will be specified.

Defining a Function

Now that you have seen how to call functions, you will learn how to define your own function. Defining a function always begins with the def keyword, followed by the name of the function, and the parentheses optionally with parameters; then the statements constituting the function come on new lines after a colon. Parameters are listed in parentheses separated by commas, and the values of these variables will be defined by the arguments during the call of the function.

Note   Function parameter or argument? When the variable names are listed in the function definition to be required at the function call, they are called *parameters* or *formal arguments*. When values are specified in the function call to be passed, they are called *arguments* or *actual arguments*. In practice, *parameter* and *argument* are often used imprecisely in an interchangeable way, and their exact meaning can be figured out from the context.

Listing 2-8 shows a function definition. It takes two parameters and returns the product of them. This function can be called as shown in Listing 2-9. The first argument (the value 1000) will be assigned to the price parameter, and the second argument (the value of 8) will be assigned to the amount parameter. The result of the function call shown in the example will be the value 8000.

Listing 2-8. Function Definition

```
def total_sum(price, quantity):
    return price * quantity
```

Listing 2-9. Call of the Defined Function

```
total_sum(1000, 8)
```

It is known from the indentation that statements belong to the function: they start with an indentation one level deeper as compared to the first line of the function definition. Lines after each other with the same indentation depth are referred to as *blocks*. Additionally, blocks can contain statements that require the following lines to be indented one more level deeper, i.e., so a novel, nested block is formed. The new block so formed is part of the block it is contained by. You can see a block in lines 2 and 3 in Listing 2-10, which are indented to the same level. This signals that it belongs to the definition in line 1. Line 4 appears on the top level, and actually lines 1 to line 4 are also considered as a block.

Listing 2-10. Blocks

```
def total_sum(price, quantity):
    total = price * quantity
    return total
extra_price = 2000
```

Caution   The space and the tab are two different characters. How many spaces are included in a tab depends on the settings. This is the reason mixed space and tab characters are not allowed to be used to indent blocks. The official recommendation is to use four spaces for every block. Compliance to this is assisted by development tools supporting the Python language: they replace tabs automatically with spaces.

A block corresponding to a function definition is called a *function body*. Statements forming the function can contain a `return` keyword and an expression after it. This statement indicates the end of the function and value of the expression will be the result of the function. When no such statement is present, the function has no results; i.e., its result is `None` as discussed earlier.

Keyword Arguments

If you want to pass arguments as keyword arguments, you can do it as shown in Listing 2-11. Parameters can be passed either as positional arguments or as keyword arguments, or as combination of the two, until the constraint of specifying positional arguments before keyword arguments is met. (There is no third variation in the example due to this constraint.)

Listing 2-11. Call of the Defined Function with Keyword Arguments

```
total_sum(price=1000, quantity=8)
total_sum(1000, quantity=8)
```

For the function definition in Listing 2-12, parameters get the default values. The parameters with default values are not allowed to be followed by parameters without default values. This is demonstrated in lines 1, 2, 3, and 4 of Listing 2-13, where for a default value the function can be called according to the previous one; this time arguments specified at the call will be passed. In lines 5, 6, 7, and 8, a single argument is specified, or no arguments are specified, and in these cases the not-specified parameters will be assigned with the default values. This is the way parameters modified on rare occasions can be made optional.

Listing 2-12. Function Definition with Default Parameters

```
def total_sum_v2(price=500, quantity=5):
    return price * quantity
```

Listing 2-13. Calling the Defined Function with Various Arguments

```
total_sum_v2(1000, 8)
total_sum_v2(1000, quantity=8)
total_sum_v2(price=1000, quantity=8)
total_sum_v2(quantity=8, price=1000)
total_sum_v2(1000)
total_sum_v2(price=1000)
total_sum_v2(quantity=8)
total_sum_v2()
```

Visibility of Names

After a variable name has been defined in the earlier examples, it can be referred to from the point of the definition. In the functions, in turn, if a variable name is defined, it cannot be referred to from "outside." If the defined total value variable name is referred to from outside the definition of the function (in our case after the definition in the line where the statements are not indented) in Listing 2-14, an error will be raised. Visibility can be summarized in three points.

- A name defined outside but before the function definition (in the block containing the definition of the function or any of the blocks containing the particular block) is visible from the function (only to access the object referenced by the name).

Listing 2-14. Function Referencing to an Outer Variable Name

```
PRICE = 2000

def total_sum_v3(quantity):
    return PRICE * quantity

total_sum_v3(100)
```

- A name is assigned to an object in the function body (inside the block belongs to the function), and a reference can be made to the name only inside the function after the assignment; the name is not visible outside the function. If the name is identical to a name defined outside the function, this new assignment will be in effect, but it does not change the assignment outside the function. In other words, by leaving the function, the object assigned to the name outside the function will be reachable with the name (it will not be overwritten; it only will be shadowed within the function). In Listing 2-15, the result of the total_sum_ v4 function call will be 30000.

Listing 2-15. Function Referencing a Shadowed Outer Variable Name

```
PRICE = 2000
def total_sum_v4(quantity):
    PRICE = 3000
    return PRICE * quantity
total_sum_v4(100)
```

- The previous two use cases cannot be mixed. That is, if a value that was also defined outside the function is assigned at any point in the function body, the reference preceding the definition in the function body will refer to the name inside the function body (an error message is given in this case indicating that no object assignments took place to the name yet, instead of accessing the value outside the function).

Functions as Parameters

Functions are objects as well, like with numbers. Therefore, a function can be given as a value of a variable name, and it can be invoked. This is useful when there is behavior to be transferred. In Listing 2-16, three methods are defined: the first and second functions calculate the discount rate from the unit price and quantity, and the third function calculates the reduced price from the unit price, quantity, and discount rate calculation function. The last two lines show examples of how the reduced_price_p can be called. The discount_30 and the discount_4p1 return a 30 percent discount value if the unit price is higher than 500 and a rate that makes one item out of free free, respectively. The reduce_price_p function calculates the total_value from the price and quantity as a first step. Then it calls its discount parameter, which is a function, to retrieve the rate of the discount. Finally, it calculates the reduced price from the total_value and discount_rate. In the first and second examples, the results are 3500 and 4000, respectively.

Listing 2-16. Function as Argument

```
def discount_30(price, quantity):
    return 0.3 if price>500 else 0
```

```
def discount_4p1(price, quantity):
    return ((quantity//5) / quantity)

def reduced_price_p(price, quantity, discount):
    total_value = price * quantity
    discount_rate = discount(price, quantity)
    return total_value * (1-discount_rate)

print(reduced_price_p(1000, 5, discount_30))
print(reduced_price_p(1000, 5, discount_4p1))
```

Definitions of Nested Functions

In the Python language, the definition of a function is considered an ordinary statement. Therefore, it may be present in a block of any depth. This is the reason why you are allowed to define a function within a function if you want to use it only in the block. Listing 2-17 shows that two short functions being defined within the functions to calculate the discounted price.

Listing 2-17. Nested Function Definition

```
def reduced_price_e(price, quantity, discount, limit = 5000):
    def total_sum():
        return price * quantity

    def d_available(total_value):
        return total_value >= limit

    multiplier = 1.0 - (discount
                        if d_available(total_sum())
                        else 0.0)
    return round(total_sum() * multiplier)
reduced_price_e(1000, 5, 0.3)
```

Functions in Practice

Three types of notations can help you when defining functions: define the parameter and return types, specify the preconditions with respect to the parameters, and include a detailed documentation string. These three notations are completely optional and primarily do not affect the behavior of a function.

Similar to the way type hints were defined for variable names in Chapter 1, the types of function parameters can be written after the name, separated by a colon. The return type of the function can be written after the function parameters, separated from it by an arrow (->).

Function can begin with a so-called documentation string (*docstring*), which provides a description of the function, that can be queried. The documentation string is a multiline comment that contains the task of the function briefly, on one line; its detailed description separated by one empty line; and finally, a description of the parameters after the Args: word.

After the documentation string, the preconditions can be represented to describe the conditions necessary for the function to work properly. These can be described with the assert statement: an assert keyword followed by a Boolean expression and optionally by an error message separated by a comma. If the preconditions expressed by the Boolean expression is not fulfilled, an error is given.

By convention, there is no space between the function name and the parentheses when calling the functions, as you saw in the examples. As to the commas, it is recommended to put a space only after the comma.

Listing 2-18 describes the process shown in Figure 2-1. Each step in the figure corresponds to one line of the example. This example demonstrates in practice how the source code can differ from the documentation. The gap can be narrowed by inserting comments into the source code identical to the ones in the figure and giving the function a name consistent with the documentation. The example uses the definitions of Listing 2-19.

Listing 2-18. Function Definition

```
def total_sum(price: int, quantity: int) -> int:
    """Calculates the total sum

    The total sum is the product of the price and quantity.

    Args:
        price: the unit price
        quantity: the quantity of the product
    Returns:
        the result of the computation, which is the value of
        the product
    """
    assert price >= 0, "the price cannot be negative"
    assert quantity >= 0, "the quantity cannot be negative"
    total_sum = price * quantity
    return total_sum

def discount_available(value: int, limit: int = 5000) -> bool:
    """Checks whether any discount is available

    Based on the limit it decides whether the discount can
    be applied

    Args:
        value: the total price of the product
        limit: a new limit if it differs from 5000

    Returns:
        True if discount is available, otherwise False
    """
```

```python
    assert value >= 0, "the value cannot be negative"
    assert limit >= 0, "the limit cannot be negative"
    return value >= limit

def reduced_price(value: int, discount: float) -> int:
    """Calculate the discounted price

    Calculates the final price according to value and discount
    variables,
    which will be the discounted price if discount is available

    Args:
        value:      the total price of the product
        discount:   amount of the discount in fraction
                    (e.g.  0.5 equals 50%)

    Returns:
        The discounted price if discount is available,
        otherwise the original value
    """
    assert value >= 0, "the value cannot be negative"
    assert 1 >= discount >= 0, "discount is not in the
    valid range"
    multiplier = 1.0 - (discount
                if discount_available(value)
                else 0.0)
    return round(value * multiplier)
```

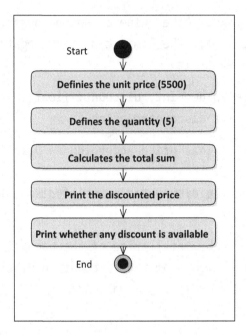

Figure 2-1. *Discount calculator*

Listing 2-19. Discount Calculator

```
PRICE: int = 5500 # unit price
QUANTITY: int = 5 # quantity
total_value = total_sum(PRICE, QUANTITY)
print('Total sum: ', reduced_price(total_value, 0.5))
print('5%' if discount_available(total_value) else 'None')
```

Advanced Details

This section describes some technical details in reference manual style and advanced concepts that may need more technical background.

Namespace and Scope

A *namespace* is an object that stores the mapping of names (variable names, function names, etc.) to objects. The outermost user-accessible namespace of the program is called the `global` namespace. In addition, there are so-called built-in namespaces that include the names of the built-in objects. The definition of the function creates a new namespace called a *local* namespace. Functions can contain further function definitions; thus, an arbitrary number of nested local namespaces can be constructed. This way, namespaces form a tree-like hierarchy, the root of which is the built-in namespace.

The *scope* of a variable name is part of the source code where a name of a namespace can refer. Resolution of a referenced name takes place by finding the assignment in the relevant local or global namespace. If this is unsuccessful, an attempt is made to find it in the next namespace outside the referenced one. The last namespace in the hierarchy is the built-in namespace. If it cannot be resolved even in this namespace, an error will be raised. Namespaces can "shadow name" each other in case an identical name is defined. This shadowing behavior can be changed by two statements: a local namespace outside of the local and global namespaces can be referenced by a nonlocal statement and a global statement (which consist of the keyword and the variable name), respectively.

Positional-Only and Keyword-Only Parameters

The function in Listing 2-20 has strange characters as parameters: / and *. These characters are not real parameters, but they have special meaning: all parameters that are preceding the / are positional-only parameters, and all parameters that are following the * signs are keyword-only arguments. The two function calls at the end of the listing are the only valid way to call the function f.

Listing 2-20. Function with Positional-Only and Keyword-Only
Parameters

```
def f(a, /, b, *, c):
    print('positional-only parameter:', a)
    print('positional or keyword parameter:', b)
    print('keyword-only parameter:', c)

f(1, 2, c=3)
f(1, b=2, c=3)
```

Variable Number of Arguments

You saw in the examples of the function call in Listings 2-4 and 2-5 that
functions can have a variable number of arguments. The notation that
can be used for this is a star put in front of the parameter's name. This
parameter will then be a special parameter that does not behave like
a simple positional parameter, but an object that will contain all the
positional arguments that were not assigned to the preceding parameters.
If there are two stars, the parameter will contain the keyword arguments
that were not assigned to the preceding parameters.

This notation also works the other way around too. If such an object
containing collected parameters is transferred with a star or with two stars,
the contained values will be expanded. In Listing 2-21, the function f call
prints "1, 2, 3" as positional parameters and then the "a: 1, b: 2, c: 3" pairs
as keyword parameters.

Listing 2-21. Variable Number of Arguments

```
def f(*args, **kwargs):
    print('positional parameters', args)
    print('keyword parameters', kwargs)

f(1, 2, 3, a=1, b=2, c=3)
```

Lambda Expression

For functions expecting another function as their parameter, the definition of the function to be passed as a parameter is frequently clumsy. The lambda function can solve this problem; it's a simple anonymous function definition containing a single expression. Listing 2-22 shows a `discount_50()` function that is transferred as an argument in line 4 to the `reduced_price_p` function, as shown in Listing 2-16. Listing 2-23 shows the replacement of the function calculating the previous discount by a lambda expression. A lambda expression in this example has two parameters: the price and the quantity to maintain the compatibility with the earlier function definition conventions, but only the quantity parameter used in the expression. As the lambda expression returns a function object, it can be written directly as a function argument of the `reduced_price_p` function.

Listing 2-22. Simple Function as Parameter

```
def discount_50(price, quantity):
    return 0.5 if quantity>10 else 0

print(reduced_price_p(1000, 15, discount_50))
```

Listing 2-23. Lambda Expression as Parameter

```
print(reduced_price_p(1000, 15, lambda price, quantity: 0.5 if
quantity>10 else 0))
```

Decorator

A *decorator* is a special notation to modify the behavior of the function. The decorator is in fact a function receiving a function as a parameter and returning a function as a result. It can be used in two typical ways: it records the obtained function into some global data structure and returns with the function originally received, or it returns with another function instead of that received as a parameter. Depending on the purpose of this new function, it can carry out operations before and after calling the original function.

A decorator is presented in Listing 2-24, which checks if the functions calculating the discount function do not calculate too high of a discount rate. If they calculate too high of a discount rate, the decorator intervenes and returns the maximum allowed discount rate. Listing 2-16 shows the definition of the function reduced_price_p used in the example.

Listing 2-24. Decorators

```
def limit_discount(discount):
    def check(price, quantity):
        pre_calculation = discount(price, quantity)
        return pre_calculation if pre_calculation<0.75
        else 0.75
    return check

@limit_discount
def discount_40(price, quantity):
    rate = 0.4 if price*quantity > 500 else 0
    return rate

@limit_discount
def sell_for_free(price, quantity):
    rate = 1.0 if quantity == 1 else 0
    return rate

print(reduced_price_p(1000, 1, discount_40))
print(reduced_price_p(1000, 1, sell_for_free))
```

Yield Statement and Asynchronous Functions

Functions that contain yield statements behave differently than the functions discussed in this chapter. They are called generator functions or co-routines, and you can find more information on them at the end of Chapter 4. These kinds of functions are the core building blocks of so-called asynchronous functions. We discuss them separately in Appendix C.

Key Takeaways

- A function call is an expression that can be denoted by writing parentheses (this is called a *function call operator*) after the name of the function. The parentheses can contain further expressions that are the arguments of the function. Calling a function means executing the statements assigned to the function. The function usually describes some calculations or changes its environment. The function call usually returns a value that can be used.

- Defining a function requires nothing more than assigning a block (list of statements) to a name. In the definition of a function, the parameters expected by the function can be listed. These parameters will be assigned to values during the call. The statements assigned to the defined function may contain a return statement, which can prescribe what object must be returned to the caller.

- It is important to note that the variables defined inside the function cannot be accessed from outside (they form a new namespace). The external variables can be accessed from the function if they meet certain criteria. If you define a variable inside the function definition with the name identical to an external variable, then this variable will be shadowed by the new variable and changing it won't have any effect on the external variable.

- The functions are also objects, like objects of the other types shown so far. Although they are defined in a different way than other objects assigned to variable names, a function is actually a variable name. Because of this, a function name can be assigned to another variable name or can be used as an argument.

CHAPTER 3

The Class: How to Model the World

"Think like an object. Of course, this statement gets its real meaning by contrast with the typical approach to software development: Think like a computer."

David West

When designing programming languages, one of the important goals is to enable the formulation of the programs in a way that is as close as possible to a real-world description of solutions. The object-oriented programming or paradigm attempts to fulfill this aim with the possibility of creating objects in the program's text that are related to objects existing in the real world. These can be either objects representing actual, existing products in the program according to Figure 3-1a, or some more abstract, technical objects, such as objects representing a file in the computer according to Figure 3-1b. In this chapter, you will gain understanding of what objects and classes are and what you can do with them.

© Gabor Guta 2022
G. Guta, *Pragmatic Python Programming*, https://doi.org/10.1007/978-1-4842-8152-9_3

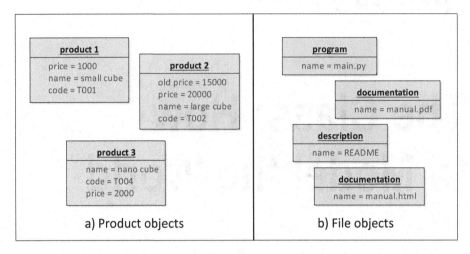

Figures 3-1a and 3-1b. *Objects*

Objects have instance variables and methods. Instance variables are variable names bound to the object. Methods, in turn, are functions describing the behavior characterizing the object. Sticking to the former example, the instance variables of the Product object can be codes, names, prices, and old prices, as well as the behaviors of the object, e.g., the product can be discounted.

Note   The term *attribute* is often used in the documentation of the Python language, meaning names after a dot. The attributes of an object are both its instance variables and its methods. Similarly, the attributes of a module are variable names, functions, and classes defined in the module. Instead of the term *instance variable*, the data attribute designation is also frequently used.

What Is a Class?

A class describes the common blueprint of similar objects. In the Python language, these classes are the types of the objects. If, for example, in an order management program products are to be represented by objects, a Product class must be defined. This definition of class describes how instance variables of the new objects are formed, and the methods that read or write these instance variables are also defined here.

Determining the classes during the development process is crucial: if the responsibilities of a class is clear, i.e., which aspects of reality are to be modeled, the program will be much easier to understand. Specifying the responsibilities of the classes can be represented only informally in the documentation, but it is the consequence of this decision that defines what kind of instance variables and methods appear in the classes. The product class would be quite different if, say, the program manages chemicals, and, besides its name, the hazard classification or storage requirements of the material would also have to be represented as the product's instance variables. See Figure 3-2.

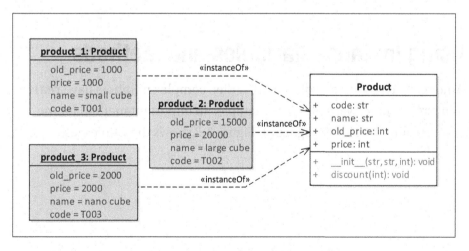

Figure 3-2. *Product objects and class*

Creating Objects

In examples cited so far, objects of a particular class have been created by defining them as values or results of expressions. Objects can also be explicitly created from classes. Object formation is called *instantiation*, as it is like creating an actual representation/instance of an abstract concept/category/generalization. When an object is to be generated from a class, parentheses are put after the class name, as if a function were to be called. Depending on the class, parameters can be specified, which usually affect the values of the instance variables of the generated object.

For example, when class int is instantiated, an int type object will be formed with a value of 0. A string can be a parameter at the instantiation of the int type, which—if containing a number—will be an integer with the same value. Listing 3-1 shows these examples.

Listing 3-1. Instantiating Objects from the Integer Type

```
INTEGER_NUMBER_0 = int()
INTEGER_NUMBER_5 = int('5')
```

Using Instance Variables and Methods

Among the types already discussed earlier, complex numbers have real and imag instance variables. For example, an important method for the complex numbers is conjugate(). Figure 3-3 shows the whole class.

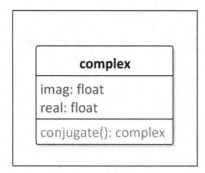

Figure 3-3. *Complex class*

The instance variables can be referenced in the following way: putting a dot after the variable name referring to the complex number and giving the name of the instance variable (`x.real` and `x.imag`, as shown in Listing 3-2).

Listing 3-2. Using a Complex Class

```
I = complex(0, 1) # 0+1j
real_part = I.real
imaginary_part = I.imag
```

In the case of methods, a pair of parentheses will follow the dot and the method name. These parentheses can remain empty (as shown for the functions), or parameters can be present in the parentheses.

```
conjugate_value = I.conjugate()
```

Defining Classes

You saw earlier how a class construct is used. Let's look at an example of how to define your own class. The class representing the product shown in Figure 3-4 is defined in Listing 3-3. The instantiation of this class is demonstrated in Listing 3-4.

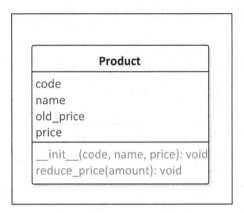

Figure 3-4. *Product class*

The definition of a class begins with the keyword class and a colon, and the block containing definitions of the class elements follows. The class usually has an initialization method named __init__(), which sets up the default state of the instance (this is similar to the concept of a constructor in other programming languages). The definition of the class contains a discount() method, which modifies the price instance variables of the Product type objects in the case of adding a discount.

The first parameter of methods defined in the class always refers to the object itself, conventionally called self. To access or modify an instance variable of the object from a method of the class, the self parameter must be used. In Listing 3-3 lines 3 to line 6 show the instance variable definitions of the Product object. In line 9, the value of the price instance variable is assigned to the old_price instance variable. In line 10, the new_price variable will take the value of the calculated price. The new_price variable is just a "normal" method variable, which is not assigned to the object in any form. The last line assigns the value of this method variable to the price instance variable. The methods of the object can be called in a similar way as instance variables are referenced: the reduce_price method could be called like self.reduce_price(0) from an additional method of the same class.

Listing 3-3. Definition of the Product Class

```
class Product:
    def __init__(self, code, name, price):
        self.code = code
        self.name = name
        self.price = price
        self.old_price = price

    def reduce_price(self, percent):
        self.old_price = self.price
        new_price = self.price * (1 - percent/100)
        self.price = round(new_price)
```

The initialization method defines the instance variables of the newly formed object by assigning their initial values. Parameters of this method will be the values specified in parentheses after the name of the class, as shown in Listing 3-4.

Listing 3-4. Instantiating from the Product Class

```
k01 = Product('K01', 'cube', 1000)
```

You can see in the first row of Listing 3-5 how to define a novel c02 object. The prices and names of object c01 defined earlier, and the newly defined c02, are printed in the second line. The price of object c01 in the third line and the name of c02 in the fourth line are changed. Both objects' names and values are printed in the last line. This example demonstrates well that although instance variables of both objects were described in the same class definition, their values are specific to the objects and can be changed independently.

Listing 3-5. Examples of Instance Variable Usage

```
k02 = Product('K02', 'small cube', 500)
print(k01.name, k01.price, k02.name, k02.price)
k01.price = 1100
k02.name = 'mid cube'
print(k01.name, k01.price, k02.name, k02.price)
```

In line 1 of Listing 3-6, the names and values of the objects are also printed. The method implementing the discount is called on line 2. This changes only the instance variables of c01 as it can be verified based on the result of print statements in the last line.

Listing 3-6. Example of Method Usage

```
print(k01.name, k01.price, k02.name, k02.price)
k01.reduce_price(30)
print(k01.name, k01.price, k02.name, k02.price)
```

An extreme case can also come up when a class contains only instance variables. A good example of this case is the Address class shown in Figure 3-5, since it consists only of instance variables: country, postcode, city, and address. Listing 3-7 shows the definition of the class.

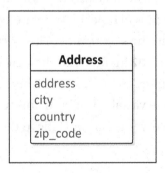

Figure 3-5. *Address class*

Listing 3-7. Address Class

```
class Address:
    def __init__(self, country, zip_code, city, address):
        self.country = country
        self.zip_code = zip_code
        self.city = city
        self.address = address
```

Objects have unique identifiers that do not change after their creation. This identifier can be queried by the id() function, the result of which is an integer. If the identifiers of two objects are equal, the objects are the same. The methods and the instance variables of the objects can be queried by the dir() function. Listing 3-8 shows the calls of the previous two functions and the output of their results.

Listing 3-8. Printing the Identifier and Attributes of an Object

```
product = Product('K01', 'cube', 1000)
print(id(product), dir(product))
```

Relationships Among Classes

The example in Figure 3-6 demonstrates a case when the customer has one billing address and one delivery address. Types of both addresses—i.e., their class—is Address.

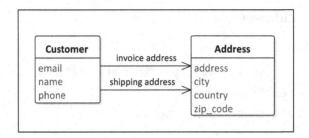

Figure 3-6. *Customer class*

The definition of the class of Address was shown in Listing 3-7. As you can see from the definition of the Customer class in Listing 3-9, references to the addresses are realized as simple instance variables.

Listing 3-9. Customer Class

```python
class Customer:
    def __init__(self, name, email, phone,
                 shipping_address,
                 billing_address=None):
        self.name = name
        self.email = email
        self.phone = phone
        self.shipping_address = shipping_address
        self.billing_address = billing_address
```

Now, we would like to model the orders in an enterprise system by classes, as shown in Figure 3-7.

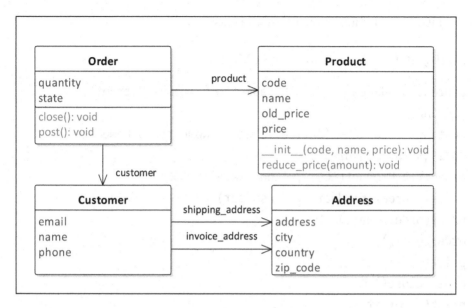

Figure 3-7. *The order and the associated classes*

Let's suppose for the sake of simplicity that only one product is ordered in a single order, in any quantity. Listing 3-10 shows the definition of the class modeling the order. The definitions of the other classes are already known from the earlier examples.

Listing 3-10. Order Class

```python
class Order:
    def __init__(self, product, quantity, customer):
        self.product = product
        self.quantity = quantity
        self.customer = customer
        self.state = 'CREATED'

    def close(self):
        self.state = 'READYTOPOST'

    def post(self):
        self.state = 'SENT'
```

Listing 3-11 shows how to use the classes.

Listing 3-11. Usage of the Class Model

```
address = Address(1020, 'Budapest', '1 Wombat Street',
"HUNGARY")
customer = Customer("Alice", "alice@wombatcorp.nowehere",
"0123456789", address)
product = Product('C01', 'Chocolate', 1000)
order = Order(product, 2, customer)
print(order.state)
order.post()
print(order.state)
order.close()
print(order.state)
```

An object first instantiated from the Address class was defined in Listing 3-7. Then an object is instantiated from the Customer class in Listing 3-9, which references the address object. In line 3, a Product class is instantiated. Finally, an object is instantiated from the Order class defined in Listing 3-3, which references both the customer and the product objects. In lines 5, 7, and 9 the state instance variable of the order is printed. In lines 6 and 8, the post and close methods of the order object are called to transition between states, respectively.

Properties

In the query of the instance variable values or in the assignment of values, it may be required to execute some operations by the object before the operation happens. In these cases, so-called properties can be defined.

The properties can return a value in the same way as an instance variable of the object, but a method will be called in the background, and the value of the property will be the output of the method. This is useful in two typical cases: 1) we do not want to store the value, since it can be computed from values of other instance variables, and 2) the instance variable refers to an object that can be modified, and we do not want it to change; therefore, a copy will be returned. Listing 3-12 shows that the property of full_address representing the full address is computed from the object's other instance variables. The name of the property is the same as the name of the method computing the property, and an @property decorator is placed before the method's definition. When a value is required to be assigned to this attribute of the object, an error will occur.

Listing 3-12. Readable Property

```
class Address:
    def __init__(self, zip_code, city, address, country):
        self._zip_code = zip_code
        self.city = city
        self.address = address
        self.country = country

    @property
    def full_address(self):
        return (f'{self.zip_code} {self.city}, '
                + f'{self.address}, {self.country}')
```

To define writable properties, in addition to the method performing the reading, another method needs to be defined with the same name, and whose decorator is the name of the method, with the setter name separated from it by a dot. This is shown in Listing 3-13, wherein the postcode is converted from a string to a number, and vice versa. The writable properties enable you to check the type of the passed-in value, for example. When the instance variable is to be deleted, a third function is needed that has the same name as the ones of the methods defined so far; its decorator begins with the same name as well and ends with a deleter after the dot.

Listing 3-13. Readable/Writable Property

```
class Address:
    def __init__(self, zip_code, city, address, country):
        self._zip_code = zip_code
        self.city = city
        self.address = address
        self.country = country

    @property
    def full_address(self):
        return (f'{self._zip_code} {self.city}, '
                + f'{self.address}, {self.country}')

    @property
    def zip_code(self):
        return str(self._zip_code)

    @zip_code.setter
    def zip_code(self, zip_code):
        self._zip_code = int(zip_code)
```

Listing 3-14 shows how to use the properties. They are accessed and modified like instance variables. In reality, the methods with the property decorator are called to get the value. The method with the zip_code. setter decorator is called to set the value of the zip_code property, and the actual value is assigned to the _zip_code instance variable.

Listing 3-14. Get and Set Properties

```
address = Address(1020, 'Budapest', '1 Wombat Street',
"HUNGARY")
print(address.full_address)
print(address.zip_code)
address.zip_code='1011'
print(address.zip_code)
```

Inheritance

Inheritance basically serves to reuse the code already written. If a new class differs from an existing one only because it extra instance variables and methods, it is not necessary to define the recurring parts again; instead, the existing class can be referenced. In this case, the existing class will be called a *base class* (or superclass), and the newly specified one will be called a *derived class* (or subclass). The nature of the connection is inheritance, and it can be said that the base class is a generalization of the derived class. The opposite is specialization.

As shown in Figure 3-8, and as demonstrated earlier in Listing 3-13, the Product class is extended to store the quantity of the product.

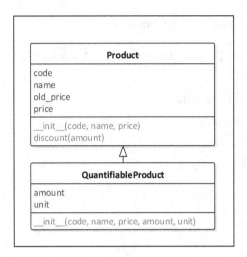

Figure 3-8. *Inheritance among classes*

The original Product class was defined in Listing 3-3. The derived class is defined by specifying the name of the base class in parentheses after the class keyword and the class name. When a base class is not specified, the object class will be the base class of the defined class. The object class implements default functionalities, and it is—directly or indirectly—the base class of all classes. The base class can be accessed by the super() function. This function is used in the example shown in Listing 3-15 to call the initialization method of the base class.

Listing 3-15. Product with Quantity Class

```
class QuantifiableProduct(Product):
    def __init__(self, code, name, price,
quantity, unit):
        super().__init__(code, name, price)
        self.quantity = quantity
        self.unit = unit
```

When defining inheritance, the derived class conceptually also needs to be a specialization of the base class. The simplest way to test this is to determine whether the derived class would behave similarly wherever the base class was present. This behavior must be transitive; namely, it should be substitutable to the place of the base class's base class. This principle is supported by the two functions shown in Listing 3-16. The isinstance() function call assists in deciding whether an object is an instance of a particular class or any one of its derived classes. In turn, the issubclass() function call assists in deciding whether another class is a derived class of a particular class. In Listing 3-16, all the queried features are true.

Listing 3-16. isinstance/issubclass Functions

```
m = QuantifiableProduct('C01', 'Chocolate', 1000, 500, 'g')
print('The m is an instance of the QuantifiableProduct class:',
      isinstance(m, QuantifiableProduct))
print('The m is an instance of the Product class:',
      isinstance(m, Product))
print('The QuantifiableProduct is a subclass of the Product
class:',
      issubclass(QuantifiableProduct, Product))
```

In the Python language, conceptual substitutability of the classes is decided based on correspondence to protocols (implicit list of required methods and properties), not only on base classes (duck typing). If a class has methods required by the protocol, it is sufficient for it to be substitutable. These protocol types can also be integrated into the type system.

The Python language supports multiple inheritance. Several base classes can be specified separated by commas. Since the order of the base classes is determined dynamically, the specification order of the base classes is considered when specifying this list. This list is stored in the __mro__ instance variable of the class, and based on this, the super() function will know what is the base class of the particular object class in the given case.

Nested Classes

Like in the case of functions, the definition of classes may also be present within other classes. These nested classes (sometimes called *inner classes*) are usually applied for storing some internal data of the containing class, as shown in Listing 3-17.

Listing 3-17. Nested Class

```python
class Order:
    class Item:
        def __init__(self, product, quantity):
            self.product = product
            self.quantity = quantity

    def __init__(self, product,
                    quantity, customer):
        self.item = self.Item(product, quantity)
        self.customer = customer
        self.state = 'CREATED'
```

```
def close(self):
    self.state = 'CLOSED'

def post(self):
    self.state = 'SENT'
```

The embedded class can be instantiated from externally too, as shown in Listing 3-18. The Product class used in this listing was defined in Listing 3-3.

Listing 3-18. Instantiating an Embedded Class

```
product = Product('C01', 'Chocolate', 1000)
item = Order.Item(product, 2)
print(item.product, item.quantity)
```

Note   Classes are also objects in the Python language, and they are instances of the type class. Classes that can create other classes are called *meta classes*. Meta classes are the derived classes of the type and not the object.

Special Methods

You saw that when specifying a number or Boolean value with the print() function that the value will somehow become a string. Up to now, when we defined an object, it was printed on the screen as a string containing the name and the identifier of the class without its instance variables. You will see how to make your own object capable of returning an informative string. In Listing 3-19 the __str__() method carrying out the conversion to the string representation is defined. The method __str__() has a counterpart called __repr__(), which is called when the resulting string will be displayed for the developer.

Listing 3-19. Special Methods for String Conversion

```python
class Product:
    def __init__(self, code, nev, price):
        self.code = code
        self.name = nev
        self.price = price
        self.old_price = price

    def reduce_price(self, percentage):
        self.old_price = self.price
        new_price = self.price * (1 - percentage/100)
        self.price = round(new_price)

    def __str__(self):
        return (f'{self.name} ({self.code}): '
                + f'{self.old_price}=>{self.price}')

    def __repr__(self):
        return (f'<Product code={self.code}, '
                + f'name={self.name}, '
                + f'price={self.price}, '
                + f'old price={self.old_price}>')
```

Methods that both begin and end with double underscores, like the previous methods, are called *special methods* in the Python language. These methods often determine the behavior of a class when they are used with built-in functions or operators applied on the object of the class. One important method is __eq__(), which performs the comparison of two objects. When we write a == b, in reality object a is performing an operation, parametrized by object b as described in Chapter 1, and a new Boolean type object is generated as a result. The previous comparison is carried out exactly as if a method call to a.__eq__(b) was in its place. Method __eq__() in Listing 3-20 works so that it compares only a single instance variable when comparing products: the product code. As its exact description and its current price are irrelevant from the point of view of the match, these instance variables will be ignored. When the object is removed, method __del__() of the class may be called, similarly to the destructor of other programming languages. Python does not guarantee that this method will be called before completing the program; therefore, it is recommended to take this into account when implementing this method.

Listing 3-20. Equals Special Method

```
class Product:
    def __init__(self, code, name, price):
        self.code = code
        self.name = name
        self.price = price
        self.old_price = price

    def discount(self, percent):
        self.old_price = self.price
        new_price = self.price * (1 - percent/100)
        self.price = round(new_price)

    def __str__(self):
        return (f'{self.name} ({self.code}): '
                + f'{self.old_price}=>{self.price}')

    def __repr__(self):
        return (f'<Product {self.name}({self.code}): '
                +f'{self.old_price}=>{self.price}>')

    def __eq__(self, other):
        if isinstance(other, self.__class__):
            return (self.code == other.code)
        return False
```

Classes in Practice

Figure 3-9 shows the model of the classes we've defined thus far with type information. In a larger system, it is important that the responsibilities of the classes are properly selected.

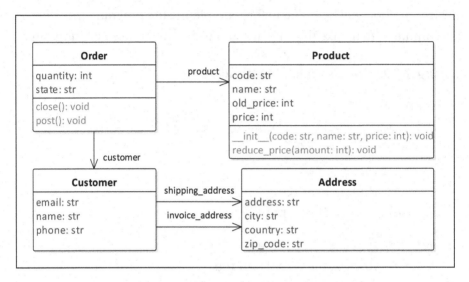

Figure 3-9. *The order and the associated classes with types*

Similarly to functions, classes can be extended with type annotations and documentation. You can see the type annotations of the instance variables from line 13 to line 16 in Listing 3-21.

You should document the class and record design decisions specifying the responsibilities of the class, as discussed in the introduction. You can see this documentation in Listing 3-21: the first line of the comment is the single-line description of the class, then the detailed information on the class follows in one paragraph, and finally a list of the instance variables beginning with the word Attributes: appears.

Listing 3-21. Class with Type Annotations and Documentation

```
class Order:
    """The data and state belong to the Order

    This order contains only a single product.

    Attributes:
        product: ordered product
        quantity: the quantity of the product
        customer: the customer
        state: state of the order; 'CREATED',
                'SENT' or 'CLOSED'
    """
    product: Product
    quantity: int
    customer: Customer
    allapot: str

    def __init__(self, product: Product, quantity: int,
                customer: Customer):
        """The state of the order is created"""
        self.product = product
        self.quantity = quantity
        self.customer = customer
        self.state = 'CREATED'

    def send(self) -> None:
        """The order sent by the supplier"""
        self.state = 'SENT'

    def close(self) -> None:
        """The order closed by the supplier"""
        self.state = 'CLOSED'
```

Advanced Details

This section describes some technical details in reference manual style and advanced concepts that may need more technical background.

Class Variables, Class Methods, and Static Methods

Python—similarly to other object-oriented languages—allows you to assign variables and methods to a class. These class variables will be specified directly in the class definition block, while class methods contain an @classmethod decorator before the method definition, and the first parameter is named cls by convention.

It can also be inferred from the parameter name that, in terms of class methods, the first parameter of the method refers to the object representing the class and has no access to the instance variables. Variables defined in the class are available for the objects as global variables related to the class. The Python language also enables you to define static methods assigned to the same class, but they do not have access to the instance variables or the class variables. The notions of the static method and static instance variable of the popular object-oriented programming languages correspond to the notions of the class method and the class variable of Python, respectively. These programming languages do not contain a notion similar to the static method in Python.

Listing 3-22 shows the class method and the static method. A single counter is defined as a class variable that will always be increased from the initialization method. This is the value of the class variable by which our class method can return. Our static method, in turn, prepares a string from the specified parameters, which will be utilized in the methods being converted to the string. It can be observed that, to produce the result, the static method processes only objects passed on to it as parameters in its call.

Listing 3-22. Order Class with Class and Static Methods

```
class Product:
    counter = 1

    def __init__(self, code, name, price):
        self.code = code
        self.__class__.counter += 1
        self.name = name
        self.price = price
        self.old_price = price

    def reduce_price(self, percentage):
        self.old_price = self.price
        new_price = self.price * (1 - percentage/100)
        self.price = round(new_price)

    @classmethod
    def product_count(cls):
        return cls.counter

    @staticmethod
    def generate_str(code, name, price, old_price):
        return f'{name} ({code}): {old_price}=>{price}'

    def __str__(self):
        product_str = self.generate_str(self.code, self.name,
                self.price, self.old_price)
        return f'{product_str}'

    def __repr__(self):
        product_str = self.generate_str(self.code, self.name,
```

```
            self.price, self.old_price)
    return f'<Product {product_str}>'

def __eq__(self, other):
    if isinstance(other, self.__class__):
        return (self.price == other.price
                and self.code == other.code)
    return False
```

Abstract Base Classes

The purpose of the abstract base classes (ABC classes) is to make possible class definitions even in cases when the common base of several classes is not suitable for instantiation. Missing properties or methods necessary for operation are marked as abstract. This means that the class, which is the specialization of this abstract base class, must define the features and methods marked as abstract. Python reserves this notation primarily for framework developers. When an abstract class is attempted to be instantiated, an error occurs. ABC classes are intended to help the work of the framework developers.

Listing 3-23 shows a Sales abstract base class, which can compute the new price of a product using the method establishing the discount rate. However, this method is abstract; how the result is computed will only be known in the class implementing the particular sales. An example for the sales class is called Sales4p1, making one free of charge out of four products and inheriting the method of computing the product's price from the Sales class. The inherited method will use the newly defined method for calculation. The exact meaning of the first line will be explained in Chapter 6. For now, it is relevant only that ABC class and the abstractmethod decorator are made accessible in the code.

Listing 3-23. Abstract Base Class

```
from abc import ABC, abstractmethod

class Sales(ABC):
    @abstractmethod
    def calculate_discount(self, price, pieces):
        ...

    def discount_price(self, price, pieces):
        value = price * pieces
        discount = self.calculate_discount(price, pieces)
        return value * (1-discount)

class Sales4p1(Sales):
    def calculate_discount(price, pieces):
        return ((pieces//5) / pieces)
```

Immutable Objects and Data Classes

If a class has a __hash__() method, it can be used as a key. The requirement is that it has to be immutable, and for each case when two objects are equal, the __hash__() method has to provide identical results (the reverse of this requirement is not required to be fulfilled). In Listing 3-24 you can see a modified version of the Address class, which is immutable and has __eq__() and __hash__() methods. As writing a correct and efficient hash function is not a trivial task, we will reuse the built-in hash function of Python: the instance variables, which are considered relevant for comparison, are packed into a tuple, and we return the hash of this tuple.

Listing 3-24. Implementing a Hash Function

```python
class Address:
    def __init__(self, zip_code, city, address, country):
        self._zip_code = zip_code
        self._city = city
        self._address = address
        self._country = country

    @property
    def full_address(self):
        return (f'{self._zip_code} {self.city}, '
                + f'{self.address}, {self.country}')

    @property
    def zip_code(self):
        return str(self._zip_code)

    @property
    def city(self):
        return str(self._city)

    @property
    def address(self):
        return str(self._address)

    @property
    def country(self):
        return str(self._country)

    def __eq__(self, other):
        if isinstance(other, self.__class__):
            return (self.zip_code == other.zip_code
                    and self.city == other.city
                    and self.address == self.address
```

```
        and self.country == self.country)
    return False

def __hash__(self):
    return hash((self.zip_code, self.city, self.address,
    self.country))
```

Classes that are used only to store data and do not have any behavior (i.e., do not have any methods) are called *data classes*. Automatic creation of initialization, string conversion, and other special methods is made possible by the @dataclass decorator. Listing 3-25 shows a version of the Address class, wherein the @dataclass decorator is used.

Listing 3-25. Data Class

```
from dataclasses import dataclass, field

@dataclass(frozen=True)
class Address:

    postcode: int
    city: str
    address: str
    country: str = field(default='HUNGARY')

    @property
    def full_address(self):
        return (f'{self.postcode} {self.city}, '
                + f'{self.address}, {self.country}')

address1 = Address(1020, 'Budapest', '1 Wombat Street')
```

This decorator constructs __init__ and all other necessary methods based on the type annotation shown in lines 7–10. The generated class will be similar to the class shown earlier in Listing 3-24. The parameter frozen=True of the decorator means that instances of the Address class

75

cannot be changed after its creation. The `country` instance variable demonstrates how it is possible to specify a default value using the `field` function. The decorator necessary to define the data class and the latter mentioned function can be made accessible using the first line of the example (for details, see Chapter 6).

Methods of Identifying Classes

One of the key issues during object-oriented modeling is how to identify objects relevant to the program. One option is to analyze the text of the existing documents: the nouns are searched in the text, and then the list is refined. Refining means identifying the synonyms and then removing the irrelevant, too general, or too specific names. Then, connections between the classes identified are analyzed, and any missing classes are identified (in most cases, these denote concepts considered trivial in the particular field; therefore, they are not mentioned in the text). The detailed description of the method can be found in the methodology called Object Modeling Technique (OMT). As the last step, this methodology recommends optimizing the classes formed here according to the technical requirements.

A CRC card is an alternative tool to identify classes. The abbreviation comes from the words of *class*, *responsibilities*, and *collaborators*. On the card, the class name is located on the top, the scope of responsibilities of the particular class is located on the left side, and the list of the cooperating classes is on the right side. The small size of the card prevents too much from being written on it for a particular class; thus, it helps to keep both the class's responsibilities and the number of classes cooperating with it low. The method's strength is that it makes the responsibility of the classes explicit and it regards a class as more than just a set of data and behaviors.

Often in the first phase of object-oriented development only abstract classes are identified that model business or domain-specific concepts. Later (at implementation time), technical classes are mixed with these classes, and the responsibilities of the business/domain-specific classes may change.

Class Diagrams

Class diagrams are the most well-known and widespread type of UML diagram. The most fundamental element in the diagram is the rectangle representing the classes; it is generally divided into three parts. The three parts contain the following textual contents: the name of the class, its instant variables, and its methods. Instant variables and methods are written in single lines each usually by indicating their type too, similar to the definition usual in programming languages. These lines can be appended by further extra information, such as the default values of the variables.

Connections between the classes are presented in the class diagram. In diagrams, associations are marked by a continuous line. Inheritance, in turn, is marked by a continuous line with an empty, closed arrowhead. If the association has a direction (the connection is essential for one of the classes only), an open arrowhead is present at the end of the line. Two important types of connections between classes exist beyond the former: dependence and containment. Dependence means that one class somehow refers to another one. This is marked by a dashed line, at the end of which an open arrowhead points to the reference. Containment denotes that one class models some part of the other class. A continuous line signifies this with a rhombus at the end of the containing class. The strength of the containment is marked by a solid or empty rhombus, depending on whether the connection is permanent (aggregation) or temporary (composition), respectively.

Key Takeaways

- In Python everything is an object: integers, strings, functions, files, or any concept modeled by the developer. The definition according to which objects are initially constructed is called a *class*. In Python, the words *class* and *type* are synonyms. Additionally, a class is also an object.

- The objects represent elements of some conceptual or physical system. The object in practice contains instance variables that represent properties of the elements and methods that are connected to these variables. Instance variables and methods are called *attributes* of an object. Objects instantiated from the same class have the same set of attributes.

- There can be many kinds of connections between the classes. A class can be defined as a refinement of an existing class. This connection is called *inheritance* as the new class inherits the attributes of the existing one. There can be dependency between the classes as one class references the attributes of other classes. The most common form of the connections between classes is that one class serves as the type of the attributes of another class. This conceptually can mean association or aggregation relation (although the technical implementation of these does not differ). If a class definition is embedded in another class definition, it means that the embedded class is intended to be used where it is defined.

- The objects implement language-specific behaviors with special attributes. For example, this is the way the behavior of operators between objects are defined.

CHAPTER 4

The Control Structure: How to Describe the Workflow

"Features of a programming language, whether syntactic or semantic, are all part of the language's user interface. And a user interface can handle only so much complexity or it becomes unusable."

Guido van Rossum

If different statements have to be executed based on various conditions or if statements need to be executed repeatedly, then so-called control structures can be used. They allow different statements to be executed depending, for example, on the value of a Boolean expression. These control structures are another important tool to enable programs to express complex behavior. In this chapter, you will learn the four main kinds of control structures of the Python language: the if statement, the match statement, the while statement, and the for statement. All these statements can be embedded into each other arbitrarily.

© Gabor Guta 2022

G. Guta, *Pragmatic Python Programming*, https://doi.org/10.1007/978-1-4842-8152-9_4

if Statement

The simplest control structure is the `if` statement. The `if` statement allows a series of statements to be executed depending on a condition formulated in a Boolean expression. This control structure is an `if` statement followed by statements depending on the condition with indentation (in the form of a block). The `if` statement begins with an `if` keyword followed by the Boolean expression and closed by a colon.

Optionally, another branch can be connected to this control structure, which runs if the condition is not satisfied. This is denoted by an `else` keyword located in the same indentation level as the `if` statement, with a succeeding colon; the statements that follow are executed if the condition is not satisfied.

You'll recall the `Product` class was defined in Listing 3-20. If the value of the discount is between the acceptable range (i.e., it is higher than 0 and lower than 99), the price of the product will be reduced. Otherwise, an error message is displayed. Figure 4-1 shows the flow.

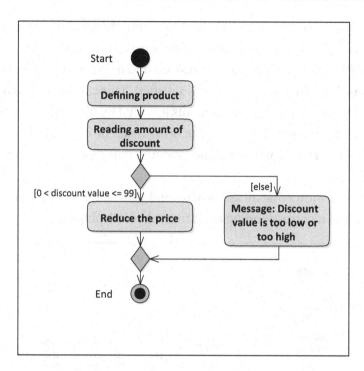

Figure 4-1. *Simple if statement*

In the first two lines of Listing 4-1, a product object is instantiated, and the extent of the discount will be asked for.

Listing 4-1. Simple if Statement

```
product = Product('K01', 'cube', 1000)
discount_value = int(input('Amount of the discount (in %)?'))
if discount_value > 0 and discount_value <= 99:
    product.reduce_price(discount_value)
else:
    print('Discount value is too low or too high')
```

The if statement may contain multiple branches guarded by different conditions. The branch following the first one starts with the elif keyword, followed by a Boolean expression and a colon with indented statements that run if the condition is satisfied. This can be repeated any number of times. With many statements guarded by different conditions, the one satisfied first will run. An else branch can be defined in this case as well to the very end, which will be executed if none of the conditions got satisfied.

Figure 4-2 shows that all kinds of invalid values are handled as separate branches, and a corresponding error message is displayed.

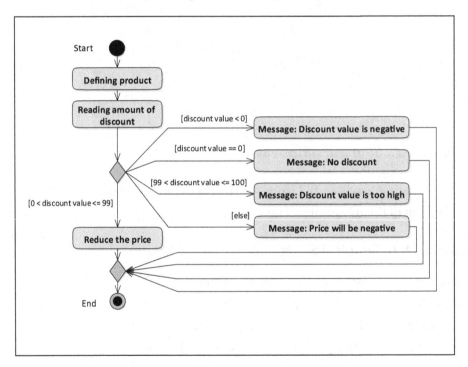

Figure 4-2. *if statement with multiple branches*

Listing 4-2 shows the corresponding Python code.

Listing 4-2. If Statement with Multiple Branches

```
product = Product('K01', 'cube', 1000)
discount_value = int(input('Amount of the discount (in %)?'))
if 0 < discount_value <= 99:
    product.reduce_price(discount_value)
elif discount_value < 0:
    print('Discount value is negative')
elif discount_value == 0:
    print('No discount')
elif 99 < discount_value <= 100:
    print('Discount value is too high')
else:
    print('Price will be negative')
```

As mentioned earlier, control structures can be embedded into each other. In Listing 4-3, the top-level if statement has a branch corresponding to the case when discount_value is not in the expected range. This branch contains an if statement that checks whether the value is too low or too high.

Listing 4-3. if Statement with an Embedded if Statement

```
product = Product('K01', 'cube', 1000)
discount_value = int(input('Amount of the discount (in %)?'))
if discount_value > 0 and discount_value <= 99:
    product.reduce_price(discount_value)
else:
    if discount_value <= 0:
        print('Discount value is too low')
    else:
        print('Discount value is too high')
```

85

match Statement

The match statement is similar to the if statement. The main difference is that it matches the resulting object of an expression to patterns to select the branch to be executed, instead of evaluating Boolean expressions. The match statement was introduced in Python 3.10. This statement starts with a match keyword followed by the expression to which the patterns are compared. After a colon, the block contains the list of the patterns. The pattern in the simplest case can be a string, integer, Boolean value, or None. Multiple patterns can be listed connected with the | symbol, which indicates an "or" connection (i.e., at least one of the patterns must match). The pattern is written between a case keyword and a colon, followed by the block that will be executed if there is a successful match.

The pattern can contain variable names and an if keyword followed by a guard condition (a Boolean expression), which can already reference the variable names. This notation of guard condition enables the practical combination of simple matching with the comparison, as shown in the if statement. What else can be a pattern will be detailed in the "Advanced Details" section.

You can also follow its functionality in Figure 4-3. In the first case, the discount_value must be equal to 0, and in this situation the "No discount" text will be displayed. In the second case, the discount_value must be equal to 1, and in this situation, the "Only 1%" text will be displayed, and the price will be reduced by 1 percent. The third case is similar to the second case with the difference that here the discount_value must be equal to 5 or 10 and the displayed text will be slightly different. The last case contains the underscore character, which means that it will match any value.

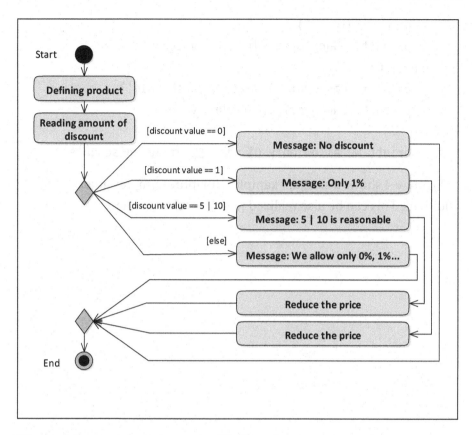

Figure 4-3. *match statement with literals*

In Listing 4-4, you can see a match statement in which one of the four cases can be selected.

Listing 4-4. match Statement with Literals

```
product = Product('K01', 'cube', 1000)
discount_value = int(input('Amount of the discount (in %)?'))
match discount_value:
    case 0:
        print('No discount')
    case 1:
```

```
        print('Only 1%')
        product.reduce_price(discount_value)
    case 5|10:
        print(f'{discount_value}% is reasonable')
        product.reduce_price(discount_value)
    case _:
        print('We allow only 0%, 1%, 5% or 10% discounts')
```

Figure 4-4 shows a similar example with more complex guard conditions. This can be also realized with a match statement.

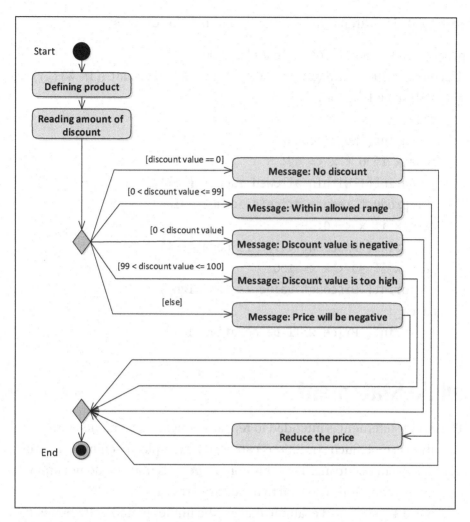

Figure 4-4. *match statement with guard conditions*

In Listing 4-5, you can see the combination of fixed patterns with guard conditions, which enables the handling of more complex cases. In the second, third, and fourth cases, the variable name x is assigned to the integer expected to be evaluated in the guard conditions.

Listing 4-5. match Statement with Guard Conditions

```
product = Product('K01', 'cube', 1000)
discount_value = int(input('Amount of the discount (in %)?'))
match discount_value:
    case 0:
        print('No discount')
    case x if 0 < x <= 99:
        print(f'Within allowed range: {x}%')
        product.reduce_price(discount_value)
    case x if x <= 0:
        print('Discount value is negative')
    case x if 99 < x <= 100:
        print('Discount value is too high')
    case _:
        print('Price will be negative')
```

while Statement

The while statement is intended to repeat a series of statements until a condition is met. Such conditions can be, for example, reaching a value or a certain event occurring. The common property is that you do not know how many repetitions will lead to the desired result.

Figure 4-5 shows an example that can be implemented in Python with the while statement.

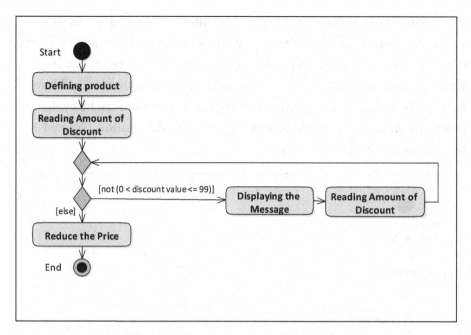

Figure 4-5. *Simple while statement*

In Listing 4-6 reading the extent of the discount is repeated until the read value falls within the expected range. When this occurs, the repetition will end, and line 6 will be executed.

Listing 4-6. Simple while Statement

```python
product = Product('K01', 'cube', 1000)
discount_value = int(input('Amount of the discount (in %)?'))
while not 0 < discount_value <= 99:
    print('Discount abount is too low or too high')
    discount_value = int(input('Amount of the discount
    (in %)?'))
product.reduce_price(discount_value)
```

91

There are two lines in the previous example where data is read: the value is read once always at the start, and second time it is read only when it was not possible to obtain a value meeting the conditions on the first try. If you wanted to read data only at one point, the read statement will have to be placed inside the loop. Additionally, the condition must be evaluated in a way that its value should be determined after the reading. Figure 4-6 represents this process visually.

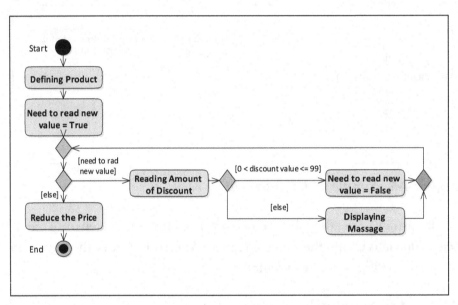

Figure 4-6. *while statement with a status variable*

The condition of the loop has been modified in Listing 4-7 so now it depends on a read_next variable. This is first true; then if the read value is found to be inside the range, it changes to false. If its value is false, the next repetition will not run. If it is not within range, its value will still be true; hence, the reading is repeated.

Listing 4-7. while statement with a Status Variable

```
product = Product('K01', 'cube', 1000)
read_next = True
while read_next:
    discount_value = int(input('Amount of the discount
    (in %)?'))
    if 0 < discount_value <= 99:
        read_next = False
    else:
        print('Discount abount is too low or too high')
product.reduce_price(discount_value)
```

The assignment expression (alias *walrus expression*) was introduced in Python 3.8, and it provides an elegant solution to the issue shown earlier. In Listing 4-8 the assignment of the level of discount located in the expression guards the while loop. The code will be more transparent; therefore, the same value giving the statement will not have to be repeated in two places or have not have to introduce a new variable to delay the evaluation of the condition.

Listing 4-8. while Statement with Assignment Expression

```
product = Product('K01', 'cube', 1000)
while not 0 < (discount_value
        := int(input('Amount of the discount (in %)?'))) <= 99:
    print('Discount abount is too low or too high')
product.reduce_price(discount_value)
```

Note that the assignment expression can be used in the while statement, if statement, and similar context and cannot be used in a stand-alone statement (as a trick it can be used in a parenthesized form, but it is not recommended).

The loop can be interrupted by a break statement. This is usually used when we want to discontinue the loop based on another condition or if it by default repeats infinitely many times. An infinitely repeating loop can be constructed by using a Boolean expression evaluated always as true (e.g., a constant of true) as a conditional expression instead of a real variable, which is changed to false at some point of the execution. Figure 4-7 shows an example.

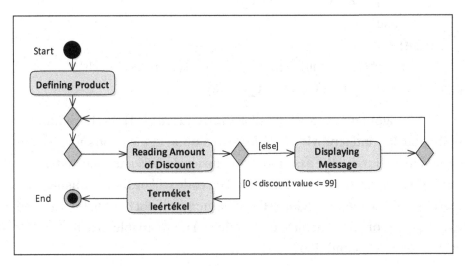

Figure 4-7. *while statement as an infinite loop*

Listing 4-9 shows the Python code for this example.

Listing 4-9. while Statement as an Infinite Loop

```
product = Product('K01', 'cube', 1000)
while True:
    discount_value = int(input('Amount of the discount
    (in %)?'))
    if 0 < discount_value <= 99:
        break
```

```
else:
    print('Discount abount is too low or too high')
product.reduce_price(discount_value)
```

The execution of the statements within the loop can be interrupted by the `continue` statement too. This aborts the execution of the following statements and starts a new cycle of the loop. This causes the re-evaluation of the loop condition, and if it is still true, the statements start to be executed again. The `continue` statement is usually used when the rest of statements must be skipped; the loop condition must be evaluated based on the changed environment or to continue an infinite loop.

Figure 4-8 shows an example of the solution being implemented in this way.

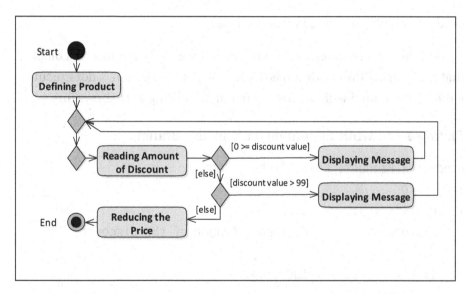

Figure 4-8. *while statement as an infinite loop (second version)*

Listing 4-10 shows the implementation of the example. This demonstrates the restart of the cycle after the execution of the `if` branches is implemented with the help of the `continue` statements.

Listing 4-10. while Statement as an Infinite Loop (Second Version)

```
product = Product('K01', 'cube', 1000)
while True:
    discount_value = int(input('Amount of the discount
    (in %)?'))
    if discount_value <= 0:
        print('Discount abount is too low')
        continue
    if discount_value > 99:
        print('Discount abount is too high')
        continue
    break

product.reduce_price(discount_value)
```

After the while statement, there can be an else keyword and a block
that runs once if the condition is not met. The else branch is not executed
if the loop is ended with the break statement. Listing 4-11 shows this.

Listing 4-11. while Statement with an else Branch

```
product = Product('K01', 'cube', 1000)
tries = 0
while tries < 3:
    discount_value = int(input('Amount of the discount
    (in %)?'))
    if 0 < discount_value <= 99:
        break
    else:
        print('Discount abount is too low or too high')
    tries += 1
```

```
else:
    print('No more try')
    discount_value = 0
product.reduce_price(discount_value)
```

for Statement

In a for loop, you can specify a repetition that corresponds to a range of values (the range can even be infinite). This statement is started with a for keyword followed by a target variable name; then an in keyword followed by an expression that generates values assigned to the variable; finally, a colon and the statements to be repeated with indentations appear. The simplest and most frequent iterator is the range function. This function makes the loop repeated by a fixed number, and the target variable name will take a value from a fixed range of numbers. The range function can have one, two, or three integer numbers as arguments.

- In the case of a single argument, the number is the repetition number (from 0 to n-1).

- In the case of two arguments, the start and end of the range are specified (from a to b-1).

- In the case of three arguments, also the size of the steps can be specified.

Chapter 5 will cover what kind of expression can be used in the for statement instead of the range function. The for statement can contain an else branch that behaves similarly to those previously covered.

The upcoming examples will show that the price change of the product is calculated for each value of discount in a specific range. Figure 4-9 shows the essence of this behavior.

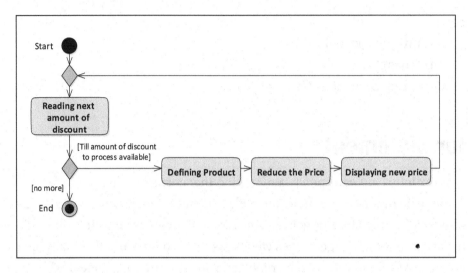

Figure 4-9. *A for statement with a fixed number of steps*

Listing 4-12 shows an example of the value of the discount running between 0 and 9. This is achieved by a range function that has a single parameter, which represents the number of steps. In this case, the first value assigned to `discount_value` is 0.

Listing 4-12. A for Statement with a Fixed Number of Steps

```
for discount_value in range(10):
    product = Product('K01', 'cube', 1000)
    product.reduce_price(discount_value)
    print('Cost of the product:', product.price)
```

Listing 4-13 shows the value of the discount running between 1 and 10. This is done by providing two arguments to the range function: the first value and the one after the last value.

Listing 4-13. A for statement with a Fixed Number of Steps with Range Arguments

```
for discount_value in range(1,11):
    product = Product('K01', 'cube', 1000)
    product.reduce_price(discount_value)
    print('Cost of the product:', product.price)
```

It is important to emphasize that in the case of two arguments the second argument is not the number of steps, but the first number that is not included in the range.

Listing 4-14 shows the discounts of 1, 3, 5, 7, and 9 percent. In this case, the range function is called with three arguments: the first value, the one after the last value, and the step size.

Listing 4-14. A for Statement with a Fixed Number of Steps with Step Size

```
for discount_value in range(1,11, 2):
    product = Product('K01', 'cube', 1000)
    product.reduce_price(discount_value)
    print('Cost of the product:', product.price)
```

This is important to emphasize that in the case of two arguments, the second argument is not the number of steps, but the first number that is not included in the range.

Listing 4-15 shows an example of what the else branch of a for statement looks like. It will be executed after the for loop successfully iterates over each value in the specified range. If the inferred price is considered too low, the if statement will break the loop, and the else branch will not be executed.

Listing 4-15. A for Statement with the else Branch

```
TOO_LOW_PRICE = 900
for discount_value in range(10):
    product = Product('K01', 'cube', 1000)
    product.reduce_price(discount_value)
    if product.price < TOO_LOW_PRICE:
        break
    print('Cost of the product:', product.price)
else:
    print('All discount values are acceptable')
```

Exception Handling

Exception handling helps to manage errors or exceptional cases separately. Thus, you do not have to insert error handling sections between statements executed during the normal executions. This helps to separate clearly which statements belong to the normal operation and which belong to the handling of exceptional or faulty operation. Errors can range from "division by zero" to "file not found." When handling an exception, the type of error or problem is signaled by the system with the instantiation of an exception object (or alternatively such an object created by the program itself as well).

The exception handling is built around four keywords: in the block after the try keyword, there is the code, which is attempted to be executed; in the blocks after the except keywords comes the statements managing the exceptional cases; the block after the else keyword contains the statements managing the nonexceptional cases; and statements in the block after the finally keyword always run. The except keyword can be followed by a class determining the type of the exception. Then it will be executed only when the exception belongs to the particular class; otherwise, it can be executed for any exception. Let's start with the simplest case in which only a try and an except branch exists.

100

Figure 4-10 illustrates this concept.

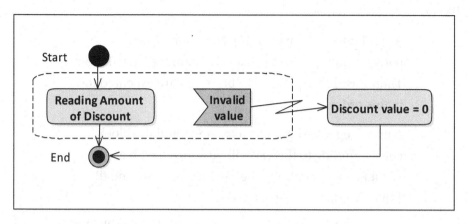

Figure 4-10. *Exception handling*

In Listing 4-16, the string read is converted to an integer. If this conversion is unsuccessful as the string contains characters other than numbers, the exception handling block is executed to set the discount value to 0.

Listing 4-16. A Simple Way to Handle Exceptions

```
try:
    discount_value = int(input('Amount of the discount
    (in %)?'))
except ValueError as e:
    print(f'Error: {e}')
    discount_value = 0
```

The except and the following block can be repeated with different exception types, but then they have to be organized in a way that the more specific class would be the preceding one. The block after the else keyword is executed if no exception occurred. The finally block will run even when the block belongs to the try statement, which can be interrupted by break, continue, or return statements.

Listing 4-17 shows a complete try statement. It can have three different execution paths.

- A valid integer is given as input, and the block corresponding to the try executes without interruption. Then the else and finally branches are executed too in this order.

- A noninteger string is given as input, and the block corresponding to the try will be aborted with a ValueError exception. Then the first except and the finally branch are executed.

- An internal error occurs in the interpreter (actually this scenario is close to impossible), and a SystemError exception is raised. Then the second except and the finally branch are executed.

Listing 4-17. A Complete Way to Handle Exceptions

```
try:
    discount_value = int(input('Amount of the discount
    (in %)?'))
except ValueError as e:
    print(f'Error converting the input: {e}')
    discount_value = 0
except Exception as e:
    print(f'Error: {e}')
    discount_value = 0
else:
    print(f'The input value is a valid integer')
finally:
    print(f'The amount of discount will be {discount_value}')
```

Triggering the exception can be achieved by the raise keyword followed by the instantiation of an exception type. This can be left out when in the exception handling block it is expected to reuse the currently handled exception object. The exception object can be instantiated from a class where the base class is the ExceptionBase. An exception can arise at any point of the program. This means that the program is stopped there and steps back to the outer block or block of the statements calling the function until it finds a point where handling of this exception took place. If there is no such point during the whole process, the program exits with an error message.

Listing 4-18 demonstrates how to raise an exception from a function. If due to any reason it cannot discount the product, the function raises an exception. To handle the conversion error of the string to a number, there is an exception handling block within the function itself. The outermost exception handling block is located around the invocation of the function.

Listing 4-18. Exception Handling with Raising an Exception

```
def reduce_price(product):
    try:
        amount = input('Amount of the discount (in %)?')
        discount_value = int(amount)
    except ValueError as e:
        raise ValueError('Not an integer')
    if discount_value > 0 and discount_value <= 99:
        product.reduce_price(discount_value)
    else:
        raise ValueError('Discount abount is too low or too high')
try:
    product = Product('K01', 'cube', 1000)
    reduce_price(product)
```

```
except ValueError as e:
    print('Modification is failed for the following
    reason:', str(e))
```

Context Management

It occurs frequently in a program that some resources are needed to be reserved and then released again. Such resources can be files or network connections that are opened and then closed. As the resource reservation and releasing pairs are easily messed up, this can be provided automatically by the context management device. A with keyword is followed by the creation of the object representing the resource to be reserved and then released. In the block that follows, the resource can be used; then when leaving the block, this is automatically closed or released.

Listing 4-19 shows how to open a file that you write to; then after leaving the block, it will be automatically closed.

Listing 4-19. Context Management

```
with open('orders.txt', 'wt') as orders_doc:
    orders_doc.write('Orders:')
```

The open function takes two parameters: a filename and a file mode (wt means writing to a text file). It returns a file object that will be assigned to the orders_doc variable name. In the second line, the Orders: string will be written in the opened files. Without the context management statement, the write statement must be followed by the method call order_doc.close() to explicitly close the file.

> ▨ **Tip**   File objects can be used to manipulate files. When opening a file by default, it is opened for reading in text mode. Files can be opened for reading (denoted with r), for reading and writing (denoted with +), or for writing (denoted with w to truncate an existing file, a to append to an existing file, or x to create a new file). The mode determines the type of the object expected by the file objects: in text mode (denoted with t) strings are read and written; in binary mode (denoted with b) bytes are expected.

The following are the five most important methods of the file object:

- The read(n) method reads n characters or bytes from the file and the entire file if the parameter is omitted.

- The readline() method reads a line from a file, but only works for the file opened in text mode.

- The write(v) method writes v into the file.

- The seek(n) method changes the position to n in the file.

- The tell() method returns the current position in the file.

Recursion

Recursion is being covered with the control structures since its behavior is similar to what can be achieved with a while statement; one has to use only a combination of a function call and an if statement. From a function, it is possible to invoke not only another function, but itself as well. This option is used typically in cases where the task can be described as an initial step and repetition of a step with changing parameters. Listing 4-20 solves recursively the following problem: how many times can a product be discounted by 10 percent to make its price lower than a given sum? A function calculating this must examine whether the current price of the product is lower than the expected price. If it is lower, it does not have to be discounted; if it is not true, these steps have to be repeated with the discounted price (i.e., the result will be that the price of the product will be reduced one more time). In this second case, the function calls itself with modified arguments. After some calls, these modifications in the arguments are expected to reach a value for which the price of the product will fall below the expected price; thus, the recursion will terminate. If the conditions are not properly specified or the step does not make the values converge fast enough to fulfill the conditions, the recursion will terminate after a certain number of calls (the default value of allowed function call depth is typically 1000).

Listing 4-20. Recursion

```
def how_many(single_pass_value, total_value,
             actual_value=None, count=0):
    print(actual_value, count)
    if actual_value is None:
        actual_value = single_pass_value
    if actual_value>=total_value:
        return count
    else:
        return how_many(single_pass_value, total_value,
                        actual_value*single_pass_value,
                        count+1)
print(how_many(1.1, 1.5))
```

Loops in Practice

For loops, it is worthy to explain in the comments the reasoning behind their expected termination and what the invariant is (a Boolean expression that will always be true upon executing the loop). As shown in Listing 4-21, the loop will terminate once an applicable discount amount is specified. During the execution of the loop, you can be sure that if the loop does not repeat more times, the amount of the discount value will be inside the range. This invariant could be useful in understanding or debugging the loop.

Listing 4-21. Comments at the Loop

```
product = Product('K01', 'cube', 1000)
read_next = True
attempts = 0
while read_next and attempts < 3:
    # Stop condition: will terminate after 3 attempts
    # Invariant: 0 < discount_value <= 99
    #            or read_next
    discount_value = int(input('Amount of the discount
    (in %)?'))
    if 0 < discount_value <= 99:
        read_next = False
    else:
        print('Discount value to high/low')
    attempts += 1
product.reduce_price(discount_value)
```

If you are unsure about the termination of the loop, you can consider introducing a counter to specify an upper number of attempts, as shown in Listing 4-22.

Listing 4-22. Loop with a Counter

```
product = Product('K01', 'cube', 1000)
read_next = True
attempts = 1
while read_next:
```

```
    # Stop condition: will terminate after 3 attempts in
    worst case
    # Invariant: 0 < discount_value <= 99
    #            or read_next
    discount_value = int(input('Amount of the discount
    (in %)?'))
    if 0 < discount_value <= 99:
        read_next = False
    else:
        print('Discount value to high/low')
        if attempts >= 3:
            raise ValueError('No valid discount value after 3
            attempt')
        attempts += 1
product.reduce_price(discount_value)
```

It is important to note that after the failed attempts the loop is left by raising an exception; this prevents the execution of the statement after the loop, which expects discount_value and does have a valid value. Naturally, a loop with a counter can be expressed with a for statement too.

Advanced Details

This section describes mostly technical details in reference manual style and some advanced concepts that may need more technical background.

Matching Classes and Other Kinds of Patterns

In the case of class patterns, you can specify patterns that can match to specific objects. The pattern contains the name of the class and in parentheses positional or keyword arguments. This syntax resembles the object instantiation syntax, but no object will be created in the current case. The sole purpose of this syntax is to describe that the expected object belongs to a certain class and to specify its expected data attribute values. The parameters are listed as keyword arguments, or in the case of positional arguments the class definition must contain a special __match__ args__ class variable. This variable must contain the list attributes relevant during the matching and their expected order in the pattern.

Listing 4-23 shows that the Product class contains the __match__ args__ variable to specify that the code, name, and price attributes can be matched and in this order. In the first case, you expect an object in which all three attributes match with values specified in the pattern. The second pattern matches an object with fixed code and value attributes, but any name. The third pattern matches an object with fixed code and name attributes, but any value. The fourth pattern matches if the object does meet any of the earlier criteria but has at least a K01 code.

Listing 4-23. match Statement with Class Patterns

```
class Product:
    __match_args__ = ("code", "name", "price")
    def __init__(self, code, name, price):
        self.code = code
        self.name = name
        self.price = price
        self.old_price = price

product = Product('K01', 'cube', 1000)
product.name = input('Default name?')
product.price = int(input('Default price?'))
match product:
    case Product('K01', 'cube', 1000):
        print('No changes')
    case Product('K01', name, 1000):
        print('Has new name')
```

```
case Product('K01', 'cube', value):
    print('Same old name, but different price:', value)
case Product('K01', name, value):
    print('Everything has changed')
```

Additional kinds of patterns can be used: lists and dictionaries (these types will be explained in the next chapter). Listing 4-24 and Listing 4-25, respectively, show examples analogous to Listing 4-23 but using lists and dictionaries.

Listing 4-24. match Statement with List Patterns

```
default_product_values = ['K01', 'cube', 1000]
default_product_values[1] = input('Default name?')
default_product_values[2] = int(input('Default price?'))
match default_product_values:
    case ['K01', 'cube', 1000]:
        print('No changes')
    case ['K01', name, 1000]:
        print('Has new name')
    case ['K01', 'cube', value]:
        print('Same old name, but different price:', value)
    case ['K01', name, value]:
        print('everything is changed')
```

Listing 4-25. match Statement with Dictionary Patterns

```
default_product_values = {'id': 'K01', 'name': 'cube',
'price': 1000}
default_product_values['id'] = input('Default name?')
default_product_values['name'] = int(input('Default price?'))
match default_product_values:
    case {'id': 'K01', 'name': 'cube', 'price': 1000}:
        print('No changes')
```

```
case {'id': 'K01', 'name': name, 'price': 1000}:
    print('Has new name')
case {'id': 'K01', 'name': 'cube', 'price': value}:
    print('Same old name, but different price:', value)
case {'id': 'K01', 'name': name, 'price': value}:
    print('everything is changed')
```

Exception Classes

As described earlier, exceptions are also objects. An exception will be instantiated from classes, the base class of which is the BaseException class or a derived class of it, the Exception. In Listing 4-26, a class named ProductcodeError is defined with two extra instance variables (the code and the message) storing error-specific information. The last line is necessary to make the message instance variable to the string representation of the exception.

Listing 4-26. Custom Exception Class

```
class ProductCodeError(Exception):
    def __init__(self, code):
        self.code = code
        self.message = f'Code {code} does not exists'
        super().__init__(self.message)
```

The exception class defined in Listing 4-26 can be raised as shown in Listing 4-27. The raised exception is also caught in the example. The last line of the listing demonstrates how the string representation of the exception can be printed.

Listing 4-27. Raising a Custom Exception

```
try:
    raise ProductCodeError('B1')
except ProductCodeError as e:
    print(f'Error: {e}')
```

Context Manager Classes

When a context is being created, an expression that yields a context manager class must be specified. The context manager classes contain two special methods: __entry__() and __exit__(). The former creates the context, while the latter destructs it.

In Listing 4-28, the DiscountAttempt class is defined that stores a reference in its instantiation to a Product type object. When entering the context managed block, it saves the instance variables of the product object, and when exiting the context, it restores the saved values.

Listing 4-28. Context Manager

```
class PriceReductionTry:
    def __init__(self, product):
        self.product = product

    def __enter__(self):
        self.price = self.product.price
        self.old_price = self.product.old_price
        return self.product

    def __exit__(self, exc_type, exc_val, exc_tb):
        self.product.price = self.price
        self.product.old_price = self.old_price

sub_cube = Product('T01', 'Substitute cube', 300)
```

```
with PriceReductionTry(sub_cube):
    sub_cube.reduce_price(20)
    print(sub_cube)
print(sub_cube)
```

Evaluating Strings

The Python language contains a built-in tool for calculating an expression stored in the form of an arbitrary string. Listing 4-29 demonstrates the evaluation of the expression covered in Chapter 1. It can be used to store the expression to be calculated in a configuration file or in other form. As the eval() makes possible the calculation of an arbitrary expression, you should be careful regarding the source of the string to be calculated so as not to give an opportunity to run malicious code.

Listing 4-29. Evaluating a String

```
eval('5000 * 2 + 2000')
```

Activity Diagram

The activity diagram is the workflow diagram of the UML standard. The activity on the diagram—denoting typically a function call or execution of an operation—is denoted by rectangles with rounded edges. The beginning and end of the process are denoted by solid and empty circles, respectively. These elements can be connected by a solid line having an open arrowhead at one end, which denotes the succession of the elements. The arrow points at the element later in time. The branches are denoted by rectangles, and conditions are written between square brackets with arrows pointing outward.

Key Takeaways

- `if` and `match` statements allow you to execute different parts of the program based on the state of the environment. If a statement evaluates a Boolean expression and the result is true, it executes a block of code. Additionally, any number of `elif` branches and a single `else` branch can be attached to the `if` statement. The `match` statement selects a branch based on the matching of a pattern to the specified object, and the branch containing the first matching pattern will be selected.

- Other important control structures are loops, namely, the `while` statement and the `for` statement. They make possible the repetition of program steps. The `while` statement executes the next block based on the result of a Boolean expression. The `for` statement expects an expression that defines how many times and for which values the next block must be executed.

- There are control structures serving special purposes. The exception handling helps to execute program blocks only in the case of errors or unexpected conditions. The objects triggering such blocks are called *exceptions*, and the developer can use the `raise` statement with an exception object to signal an error or unexpected condition.

CHAPTER 5

The Sequence: From Data to the Data Structure

"Computer programs usually operate on tables of information. ... In its simplest form, a table might be a linear list of elements, when its relevant structural properties might include the answers to such questions as: Which element is first in the list? Which is last? Which elements precede and follow a given one? How many elements are in the list? A lot can be said about structure even in this apparently simple case ..."

Donald E. Knuth

Several data types have been described so far, such as numbers, Boolean values, and strings. In addition, you learned how to define your own types, i.e., classes. In the case of the Order class, you might realize that allowing it to reference more than one product (or an arbitrary number of products) in the model would be useful. To make this possible, you need a notation to reference the objects with an index number or other identifiers. Such classes or types able to reference a variable number of objects—based on some structural property—are called *data structures*.

© Gabor Guta 2022
G. Guta, *Pragmatic Python Programming*, https://doi.org/10.1007/978-1-4842-8152-9_5

When elements are represented after each other in a row and you can refer to them based on their position in the row, they are called *sequences*. Two important sequence types exist in the Python language: one is the list; the other is the so-called tuple. Lists can be modified, while tuples have a fixed number of elements and cannot be modified after creation. The sequence is rather a natural concept when you think of the many situations when data to be processed is listed sequentially.

For the sequence, the succession of the objects provides the structure of the class. Data structures have another important group in addition to the sequences. In that group, it matters only whether a reference by a key can be made or not to a particular object. The two most important examples of this kind of structuring of data are the dictionary and the set. They will be examined in this chapter too.

Lists and Their Operations

Objects to be put into a list should be written in square brackets ([ ]) and separated by commas. To read objects from the list—which is also called "accessing an object"—you have to know their index numbers. As a list can be modified, any number of new elements can be added later or can even be deleted from it.

Listing 5-1 creates a list with five product names, as depicted in Figure 5-1.

Listing 5-1. List of Product Names

```
product_codes = ['cube', 'small cube', 'tiny cube',
                 'large cube', 'XL cube']
```

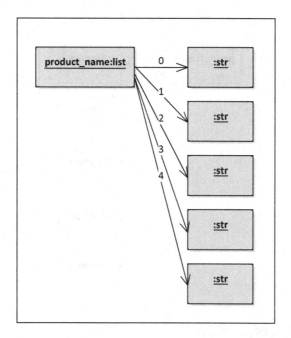

Figure 5-1. *List of product names*

Lists can contain more complex elements, for example Product objects. Listing 5-2 creates a list with five Product objects (the Product class was defined in Listing 3-20), as shown in Figure 5-2.

Listing 5-2. List of Products

```
products = [Product('K1', 'cube', 1000),
           Product('K2', 'small cube', 500),
           Product('K3', 'tiny cube', 50),
           Product('K4', 'large cube', 1500),
           Product('K5', 'XL cube', 5000)]
```

117

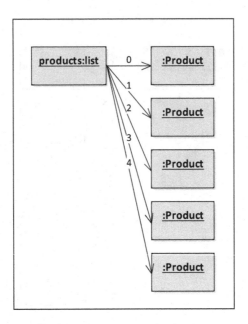

Figure 5-2. *List of products*

Finally, Listing 5-3 creates a list containing elements of different types, as shown in Figure 5-3. Such a list is usually used as a record, and variables are stored in certain positions. In our example, the code of the product is stored in the first position, the product name is stored in the second position, and the Product object is in the last position. However, this is generally not recommended as classes provide a much cleaner structure.

Listing 5-3. List of Mixed Type Objects

```
mixed_list = [
    1,
    'cube',
    Product('K1', 'cube', 1000)
]
```

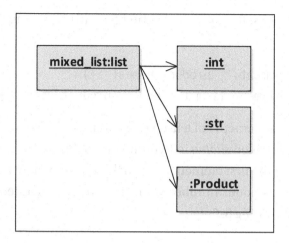

Figure 5-3. *List of mixed type objects*

Elements of the list can be accessed by writing their index number after the variable names in square brackets (this is also frequently called *indexing* or *subscript notation*). In most programming languages, the first element gets the 0 as the index number, the second one the number 1, the third one the number 2, and so on. This index number is always an integer or an expression, the result of which is an integer. Listing 5-4 shows how to access the first, second, and fifth elements. When the index number is negative, the index number of the elements is counted from the end of the list. In Listing 5-5, the -1 refers to the last element, and the -5 refers to the first one. The positive index value can be calculated by adding the length of the sequence to the negative index value.

Listing 5-4. Accessing Objects in the List

```
print('First element:', product_names[0])
print('Second element:', product_names[1])
print('Fifth element:', product_names[4])
```

Listing 5-5. Accessing Objects in the List with Indexing from the End of the List

```
print('Last element:', product_names[-1])
print('Fifth element from the end:', product_names[-5])
```

A range of the elements of a list, i.e., a sublist, can also be accessed (this operation is called *slicing* in Python). To do this, you must specify the index number of the first element to be included in the new list, separated by a colon from the index number of the first one not included in the new list, as shown in Listing 5-6.

Listing 5-6. Sublists of a List

```
print('Elements from the index 0 to the index 2:',
product_names[0:3])
print('Elements from the beginning to the index 2:',
product_names[:3])
print('Elements from the index 2 to the end:',
product_names[2:])
```

This operation is called *slicing*. When the index numbers preceding or following the colon are omitted, the new list is meant from the first or last element. When an additional colon is specified inside the square brackets, the number of steps can be specified after the second colon. Listing 5-7 shows an example of stepping by two in the first expression, the result of which is the partial list consisting of elements with index numbers of 1 and 3, respectively. An example is shown for the backward stepping by two in the second expression. This time the initial and final index numbers must be specified interchanged, the result of which is a new list consisting of elements with the index numbers 3 and 1, respectively. When there is only a single colon in the square bracket, a partial list identical to the original list will be obtained.

Listing 5-7. Sublists of a List with Increments

```
print('Every second elements from the index 1 to index 3:',
    product_names[1:4:2])
print('Every second elements reversed from the index 3 to
index 1:',
    product_names[3:0:-2])
print('All of the elements:', product_names[:])
```

The length of the list (the number of elements in it) can be queried by the len() built-in function. As shown in Listing 5-8, it is possible to append by the append() and extend() methods, depending on whether one element or another list is appended. In the case of these methods, the change takes place in the existing list; in other words, they create an in-place modification of the list. When a new list is intended to be created by appending two existing ones, using the + (concatenation) operator is expected.

Listing 5-8. List Operations

```
print('The product names list:', product_names)
print('Length of the products list:', len(product_names))
product_names.append('pluss cube')
product_names.extend(['cube v2.0', 'cube v3.0'])
print('The list after the inplace modification:',
product_names)
print('The concatenated lists:', product_names + ['CUBE 4++'])
print('The product names list:', product_names)
```

The deletion of the list elements can be carried out by the del keyword. The remove(x) method of the list can be used to remove elements based on their values. For example, as shown in Listing 5-9, the first element is removed from the product_names in line 2 and the element with the value cube v2.0 in line 3.

Listing 5-9. Deleting from a List

```
print('The product names list:', product_names)
del product_names[0]
product_names.remove('cube v2.0')
print('The product names list:', product_names)
```

Lists can be easily processed in a for loop. Namely, sequences can also be present instead of the range object. In this case, the cycle variable of the for takes the values of this sequence. Listing 5-10 shows how to print each product of a list.

Listing 5-10. Processing a List in a Loop

```
print('Products for sale:')
for product in products:
    print(product)
```

Lists, like the numbers, are also objects; therefore, they can be elements of other lists, too. (A list can also be added to itself technically, but this doesn't make too much sense.) It also must be noted that these embeddings can be arbitrarily deep.

Listing 5-11 shows a list, and the elements of the list are other lists. These embedded lists contain groups of product names. In the first print call, the first group is displayed. Then in the next print call, the first element of the first group is displayed. In this example, you can see that the embedded list element is accessed the same way as the top-level list element; in other words, the first index operator returns the first list, and the second index operator its first element. After the first two print statements, the second list is modified. After selecting the second element of the top-level list, a new element is appended to the accessed list object. After that, the second list (the group of medium-sized cube names) is printed. Finally, the two elements of the second group are printed.

Listing 5-11. Embedding a List

```
product_name_groups = [
    ['small cube', 'tiny cube'],
    ['cube'],
    ['large cube', 'XL cube'],
]
print('First group:', product_name_groups[0])
print('First element of the first group:',
      product_name_groups[0][0])
product_name_groups[1].append("Cube M+")
print('2nd group:', product_name_groups[1])
print('First and second elements of the 2nd group:',
      product_name_groups[1][0], 'and',
      product_name_groups[1][1])
```

As you can see, the list is also an object, the type of which is list. Hence, it can also be generated by directly instantiating the list() expression. From among the types shown so far, this is the first embedded type that is mutable (i.e., it can be modified).

Processing of a List

The Python language has a so-called list comprehension statement that generates a list from a list-like object. This statement is usually applied to execute some operation on the objects in the existing list and place the result objects in a new list. In the list comprehension statement, only the operations that have no side effects are recommended. The list comprehension statement consists of the following elements written between square brackets ([ ]): an expression, for keyword, target variable name, in keyword, and iterator object. This has a meaning similar to the

123

for statement: the target variable takes the next element of the iterator and calculates the expression before the for keyword. The result of the calculation is placed in a newly generated list, which will be the result of the whole list comprehension expression.

In Listing 5-12, from line 1 to line 3, from the product type objects a product name list is generated with the notation previously covered. The same thing is performed in line 4, but with the "list comprehension" notation. The two equivalent lists are printed in line 5 to enable verification of their equivalence.

Listing 5-12. Processing a List

```
names = []
for product in products:
    names.append(product.name)
names_v2 = [product.name for product in products]
print(names, names_v2)
```

Let's look at examples of how to make use of list comprehension. List comprehension that is identical to the previous example is shown separately in Listing 5-13 (only the variable name product was renamed to p).

Listing 5-13. List Comprehension

```
[p.name for p in products]
```

Listing 5-14 shows that extra filtering is added to the processing: it will be part of the resulting list only if the expression after the if is evaluated as true.

Listing 5-14. List Comprehension with Condition

```
[p.name for p in products
        if p.price >= 1000]
```

Listing 5-15 shows how to prepare the product name pairs from all combinations of the elements of the two lists where the price of the first product is lower than that of the second. This example produces all combinations without the if keyword as follows: the first variable of the pair (p), which first references the first product object, will "step" to the next object only after all the objects were enumerated as the value of the second variable (p2); then objects are enumerated as the value of the second variable repeatedly after the first variable takes a new value as long as the last object is selected for the first variable.

Listing 5-15. List Comprehension with Multiple Lists

```
[(p.name, p2.name) for p in products
                   for p2 in products
                   if p.price < p2.price]
```

Operations on sequences are efficiently supported by various built-in functions. When you want to know whether all elements in a list are true or not, you can use the all() function to query; and when the question is whether the sequence has at least one true element, you can use the any() function. When using it in connection with a list comprehension to examine an arbitrary feature, as shown in Listing 5-16, you can figure out whether a particular condition is satisfied or not for all elements or at least for one of them.

Listing 5-16. Operation on Lists of Boolean

```
print('All names contains "cube":',
      all(['cube' in p.name for p in products]))
print('Any names contains "cube":',
      any(['cube' in p.name for p in products]))
```

Listing 5-17 shows functions applicable for lists of number objects: the selection of the maximum and minimum elements and the calculation of the total amount.

Listing 5-17. Operation on Lists of Numbers

```
print('Highest price:',
      max([p.price for p in products]))
print('Lowest price:',
      min([p.price for p in products]))
print('Avarage price:',
      sum([p.price for p in products])/len(products))
```

When using lists as iterators, two useful functions are worth mentioning. One is the enumeration function, which generates another iterable object from an iterable object; it will contain pairs of an index number of the element and the original element. The other is a zip function, which is able to join the iterable objects specified as a parameter to a single iterable object. This object returns with the next elements of the objects specified as parameters as a tuple of the elements. The iterator object created by the zip function is able to produce as many elements as the shortest of the function's iterable parameters. Some cases for the use of these functions were shown in Listing 5-18. A numbered enumeration of the products is shown on lines 1 and 2. The number that should be assigned to the first enumerated element can be specified in the start parameter. An example is shown on lines 3–5 for how to process elements of a list in pairs without an indexing operator: the original list is appended to its copy shifted by one element. The difference between the pairs and direction of the relation is displayed.

Listing 5-18. Enumerating and Zipping Lists

```
for i, p in enumerate(products, start=1):
    print(i, p.name)
for p1, p2 in zip(products, products[1:]):
    print(abs(p1.price-p2.price), p1.name,
          '<' if p1.price < p2.price else '>', p2.name)
```

Tuples

The tuples (or they are also called *ordered lists* or *records*) are read-only lists with N elements. The tuples with two elements will be called *pairs* in the book, those with three elements *triples,* and so on. A tuple's definition is similar to that of a list, but round parentheses are used instead of square ones. The same operations can be used as operations to read the list. Listing 5-19 shows a definition of a pair.

Listing 5-19. Tuples Within Parentheses

```
products_fix = (Product('K1', 'cube', 1000),
                Product('K2', 'small cube', 500))
```

The Python language makes it easy to use tuples in its syntax because it is not necessary to write the brackets in certain cases. As shown in Listing 5-20, with two Product objects separated by a comma, you get a tuple. This behavior can be checked according to Listing 5-21 by reading its first element (or alternatively querying its type by using the type() function).

Listing 5-20. Tuples Without Parentheses

```
products_fix2 = Product('K1', 'cube', 1000), \
                Product('K2', 'small cube', 500)
```

Listing 5-21. Accessing Objects in a Tuple

```
products_fix2[0]
```

This separation by comma notation can also be used to unpack sequences. If the tuple defined previously (or any other sequence type) is assigned to variable names separated by commas, the first variable gets the first element, and the second variable gets the second one. The number of the variables and the number of the sequence elements should be the same. If the exact length of the sequence is unknown, a star can be placed before the last variable name, which will contain the rest of the sequence not assigned to variables. In line 1 of Listing 5-22, the unpacking of a sequence with two elements is shown. The unpacking of a previously defined list with five elements is shown on line 2, the way the first two elements are assigned to variables k_1 and k_2, while the rest of the list will be contained by the k_rest variable.

Listing 5-22. Unpacking Sequences

```
k1, k2 = products_fix
k1, k2, *k_rest = products
```

The unpacking notation can be also used in for statements, as you will see in the following sections.

Tip   Tuples with a single element can also be created. Since the notation of this coincides with the notation of the parenthesized expression, a comma should always be placed after a single element. For example, a tuple with a single element (containing one product) is defined by the product notation.

Dictionaries

Dictionaries are useful types when elements are intended to be referenced by an arbitrary value (usually called a *key*) instead of their index numbers. You can define a dictionary by listing the key-value pairs in braces, separating a key from a value by colons, and using a comma between the different key-value pairs. It is important that the keys are immutable. Five key-value pairs are listed in Listing 5-23. The keys are strings containing two characters, while the values are Product objects.

Listing 5-23. Dictionaries of Products

```
codes = {'K1': Product('K1', 'cube', 1000),
         'K2': Product('K2', 'small cube', 500),
         'K3': Product('K3', 'tiny cube', 50),
         'K4': Product('K4', 'large cube', 1500),
         'K5': Product('K5', 'XL cube', 5000)}
```

Listing 5-24 demonstrates that the reference is made to the dictionary element with a key instead of a number, as you saw with lists.

Listing 5-24. Accessing Objects in a Dictionary

```
codes['K1']
```

Assigning a value to a key of a dictionary if a key has already been taken causes the value to be overwritten; otherwise, it will be added as a new element. Modification of the dictionary is shown in the first line in Listing 5-25, while addition of a new key-value pair to the dictionary is shown in the same example in line 2.

Listing 5-25. Modifying Values of a Dictionary

```
codes['K2'] = Product('K2', 'mini cube', 600)
codes['K6'] = Product('K6', '+ cube', 1000)
```

You can form the union with the | operator, as shown in Listing 5-26. Elements of the dictionary can be updated also in groups by the update method, as shown in lines 1 to 4 of Listing 5-27. Lines 5 to 8 have the same effect, but an operator is used.

Listing 5-26. Union of Dictionaries

```
new_codes = {'K1': Product('K1', 'starter cube', 900),
             'K10': Product('K10', 'premium cube', 90000)}
codes | new_codes
```

Listing 5-27. Updating Dictionaries

```
codes.update({
    'K7': Product('K7', 'cube v2.0', 2000),
    'K8': Product('K8', 'cube v3.0', 2900)
})

codes |= ({
    'K17': Product('K17', 'cube v12.0', 12000),
    'K18': Product('K18', 'cube v13.0', 12900)
})
```

When you want to process all elements in the dictionary like a sequence in a for statement, three methods can be used. These three different methods to iterate through the dictionary are as follows: the key() enumerates the keys, the values() method enumerates the values, and the items() enumerates the key-value pairs. The order of the enumerated values is the same as the order of their addition to the dictionary. A dictionary that retains the order of addition to the dictionary is called an *ordered dictionary*. Listing 5-28 shows an example that iterates over the keys of the codes dictionary and reduces the price of the products by 3 percent.

Listing 5-28. Enumerating Dictionary Keys

```
for k in codes.keys():
    codes[k].reduce_price(3)
    print(f"New price of the product with {k} code is
    {codes[k].price}")
```

In Listing 5-29 the same functionality is achieved, but this example enumerates the values of the dictionary entries.

Listing 5-29. Enumerating Dictionary Values

```
for p in codes.values():
    p.reduce_price(3)
    print(f"New price of the product with {p.code} code is
    {p.price}")
```

Finally, in Listing 5-30 the same functionality is achieved by enumerating key-value pairs.

Listing 5-30. Enumerating Dictionary Key-Value Pairs

```
for k, p in codes.items():
    p.reduce_price(3)
    print(f"New price of the product with {k} code is
    {p.price}")
```

Not only lists but dictionaries can be generated similarly to the list comprehension. The difference compared to the notation of the list comprehension is that the dictionary comprehension requires the usage of braces instead of the square parentheses, and there must be independent expressions for the calculation of the key-value pairs, separated by a colon. In Listing 5-31, a dictionary is generated from the list of `Product` type objects, which contains codes assigned to the product names.

Listing 5-31. Dictionary Comprehension

```
{p.code: p.name for p in products}
```

Sets

The behavior of the set type is equivalent to the mathematical set concept. You can also think of a set as a dictionary without a value, which corresponds to its notation. Listing 5-32 shows three set definitions.

Listing 5-32. Sets of Strings

```
SIZES = {'LARGE', 'SMALL'}
OTHER = {'DISCOUNTED', 'LASTONES'}
THE_PRODUCT = {'LARGE', 'DISCOUNTED'}
```

The same operations can be performed between sets, which we are used to perform between mathematical sets. The operations shown in Listing 5-33 are in this order: union, section, and difference. And the same operation is shown in Listing 5-34 only realized with method calls.

Listing 5-33. Operations Between Sets with Operators

```
labels = SIZES | OTHER
the_size = THE_PRODUCT & SIZES
print(the_size)
opposite = labels - THE_PRODUCT
print(opposite)
```

Listing 5-34. Operations Between Sets with Methods

```
labels = SIZES.union(OTHER)
the_size = THE_PRODUCT.intersection(SIZES)
print(the_size)
opposite = labels.difference(THE_PRODUCT)
print(opposite)
```

A set is a modifiable type; therefore, if it is intended to be used as a key, it should be converted to a read-only type. Read-only sets are notated by the frozenset type. The simplest way to create them is to convert existing sets, as shown in Listing 5-35.

Listing 5-35. Immutable Sets as Keys

```
categories = {
    frozenset({'DISCOUNTED', 'SMALL'}),
    frozenset({'DISCOUNTED', 'LARGE'}),
    frozenset({'LARGE'}),
    frozenset({'SMALL'}),
    frozenset()}
frozenset({'LARGE', 'DISCOUNTED'}) in categories
```

Tip   In the definitions of the list, it is allowed in Python to have an extra comma after the last element in tuples, dictionaries, and set values. This is useful because if each element is present on a separate line, there is no need to deal with correcting the previous line in the case of adding an extra item or removing an item at the end of the list.

Copying Sequences

It is important to be aware that these data structures can be modified. Since variable names are just references to the objects in Python, in the case of an assignment to another, the variable name refers to the same object. This means that after the modification through referencing with the new variable name, the modification will be visible also when accessing the object with the original variable name.

If you want to assign a copy of an object to a new variable name, a new object has to be instantiated in a way that the content of source is copied. Objects in the data structure generated in this way continue to be identical, but now, in turn, in case the data structure itself got changed, this will have no effect on the original data structure. This means that new elements can be added, elements can be removed, and the order or other structural features can be changed, and they will apply only to the newly instantiated object. Listing 5-36 demonstrates this theory and shows various ways of copying lists. In the assignment in line 2, the object referenced by the b variable name is identical with that referenced by a. In the assignment in line 3, the object referenced by the c variable name is a copy of the object referenced by a. An alternative notation for copying the a list is shown in line 4. This alternative notation means that a partial list is generated from the list that contains the elements from the first element of the list to the last one. The identity of the references is examined in the last line: based on the above, a and b are identical, while the rest are different.

Listing 5-36. Copying Lists

```
a = ['S cube', 'M cube', 'L cube']
b = a
c = list(a)
d = a[:]

print('Do a and b reference to the same object?', a is b)
print('Do b and c reference to the same object?', a is c)
print('Do a and d reference to the same object?', a is d)
```

Since the objects referenced by the copied lists are identical, any changes in the mutable elements will continue to be visible in the source data structure. Thus, the previous copy mechanisms are called a *shallow copy*. Listing 5-37 shows the effect of the shallow copying mutable objects. In this example, you are creating a list from lists of strings called orig_names and shallow copying it to the list copied_list. Elements are added to the list orig_names and its last embedded list. When the lists are printed, the first addition is visible only in the original list, while the second addition is also visible in the copied list. This is because even the list copied_name is a new list; it references the same objects as the original list, and some of the referenced elements were mutable.

Listing 5-37. Copying Lists with Mutable Elements

```
orig_names = [['XS cube', 'S cube'], 'M cube', ['L cube',
'XL cube']]
copied_names = orig_names[:]
orig_names.append('+ cube')
orig_names[2].append('XXL cube')

print('Original list:', orig_names)
print('Copied list:', copied_names)
```

If you want to prevent this behavior, you have to duplicate all of the elements, not just the top-level object. This is called a *deep copy*; you can find further information in the "Advanced Details" section.

Sequences in Practice

For data structures, what is worth documenting are the constraints on the elements in the comments (for example, the price of every product is at least $100 USD) or their layout (for example, the list always contains an element, and they are ordered). Listing 5-38 shows three comments on lists: the second comment is useful for its reader as it confirms the properties of the list, which can be inferred from the initial values; and the first and third ones are useful as the described properties are hard to guess from the values.

Listing 5-38. Commenting Sequences

```
# unordered positive integers
daily_sales = [1, 2, 4, 7]
# monotonically increasing positive integers
cummulative_daily_sales = [1, 3, 7, 14]
# unordered signed integers
changes_in_daily_sales = [1, 1, 2, 3]
```

Advanced Details

This section describes mostly technical details in reference manual style and some advanced concepts that may need more technical background.

Iterable Objects

Iterability as a feature of objects has been mentioned several times without its exact definition. A class is *iterable* if it is able to return a so-called iterator object; i.e., it has an __iter__() method. Iterator objects, in turn, are objects that have a __next__() method giving a "next" element. The iterator objects also have a method, similarly to the iterable classes; this method is able to return an iterator—in this case, it means itself. Listing 5-39 shows an example.

Listing 5-39. An Iterable Class

```
class Items:
    class Item_iter:
        def __init__(self, item):
            self.i=iter(item)
        def __iter__(self):
            return self
        def __next__(self):
            return next(self.i)

    def __init__(self, items):
        self.items = list(items)

    def __iter__(self):
        return Items.Item_iter(self.items)
```

Listing 5-40 shows an instantiation of the Items class. Then a for statement prints the elements of the items object.

Listing 5-40. Iteration with for Statement

```
items = Items(('K1', 'K2', 'K3'))
for item in items:
    print(item)
```

Finally, Listing 5-41 shows an emulation of the behavior of the for statement: an iterator corresponding to the items object is retrieved. Then the objects emitted by this iterator are printed until no StopIteration exception is raised.

Listing 5-41. Manual Iteration

```
item_iter = iter(items)
print(next(item_iter))
print(next(item_iter))
print(next(item_iter))
print(next(item_iter))
```

Deep Copy of Data Structures

If you want to fully retain a data structure before modification, you have to create a so-called deep copy. This technically means that not only a single object has to be copied, but all the objects it refers to. This has to be repeated recursively if the referenced objects refer to further objects. Python has built-in tools to accomplish this, as shown in Listing 5-42. The meaning of the first line will be explained in Chapter 6. The copy function creates a shallow copy, while the deepcopy function creates the deep copy. At the end of the listing, it can be verified from the results of the print statements that the deep copied list was not affected by any of the modification of the original data structure.

Listing 5-42. Shallow and Deep Copy

```
from copy import copy, deepcopy
orig_names = [['XS cube', 'S cube'], 'M cube', ['L cube',
'XL cube']]
shallow_copied_names = copy(orig_names)
deep_copied_names = deepcopy(orig_names)
orig_names.append('+ cube')
orig_names[2].append('XXL cube')

print('Original list:', orig_names)
print('Shallow copied list:', shallow_copied_names)
print('Deep copied list:', deep_copied_names)
```

Generator Functions and Coroutines

Generator functions are functions that produce a sequence of return values instead of a single return value. Syntactically it looks like a function that returns a value, and then it continues its execution. This is realized technically by the functions themselves returning an iterable generator object. The function body will be executed when the next element is requested from the generator object. The generator object stores the state applicable in the moment of returning the element, and this state is used to produce the next element. Generator functions have the advantage against the precalculated lists that they do not have to reserve memory, because they always calculate only the next element. After returning the last element, the request of the next one raises a `StopIteration` exception.

Listing 5-43 shows a generator function, the result of which are values of a particular `Product` discounted by different amounts.

Listing 5-43. A Generator Function

```python
def discount_price():
    for discount_value in range(10):
        product = Product('K01', 'cube', 1000)
        product.reduce_price(discount_value)
        yield product.price

for price in discount_price():
    print(price)
```

Figure 5-4 shows the actual execution of the discount_price generator function. The vertical lines correspond to objects, and the vertical lines represent function calls (and returns). The time flows from the top of the figure to the bottom. The iterator object appears first in a lower position as it is created only at that point after the discount_price() generator function was called.

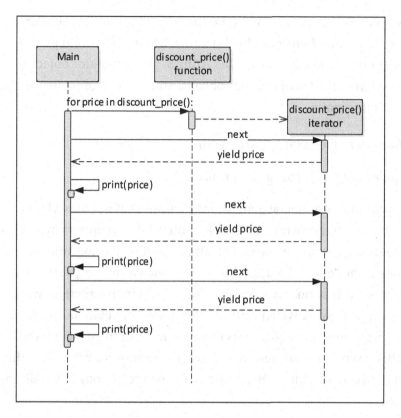

Figure 5-4. *Execution of a generator function*

Note   The `range` class and the `enumerate()` and `zip()` functions shown previously are all realized by a generator function. The advantage of this is they don't have to calculate elements of the sequence in advance, and they do not occupy space in memory.

A generator function can also be specified by a notation similar to that used in list comprehension. The difference will be that round parentheses are used instead of square ones. In Listing 5-44, a generator object is produced from the list of Product objects, and this will generate the code-product name pairs.

Listing 5-44. Generator Expression

```
((p.code, p.name) for p in products)
```

Coroutines are special generator functions that not only yield a value, but also receive one. Recent Python versions support two kinds of coroutines: generator-based coroutines and native coroutines. The first one is the "earlier" feature, which contains a yield expression or a yield from expression. This variant is discussed in this section, while the relatively new native coroutine is discussed in detail in Appendix C. You must note that coroutines form the basis of the programs with the so-called asynchronous behavior. Listing 5-45 shows a coroutine, the result of which are values of a particular Product discounted to different extents.

Listing 5-45. A Coroutine

```
def discount_price():
    product = Product('K01', 'cube', 1000)
    discount_value = 0
    while True:
        product.reduce_price(discount_value)
        discount_value = yield product.price
        if discount_value is None:
            return
```

Functional-Style Manipulation of Lists

The map function provides a functionality similar to the list comprehension. The filter function is able to create a list from an iterable expression that contains only the elements fulfilling a condition. In Listing 5-46, the function map() applies the function specified as the first parameter to each element of the iterable expression specified as the second parameter and generates a new list from them. The filter() function receives a Boolean function as a first parameter and an iterable object as a second parameter. If the Boolean function evaluates to true on the value returned by the iterable object, the value will be included in the list to be generated, otherwise not.

Listing 5-46. Functions for Functional-Style List Processing

```
(list(filter(lambda p: p.price >= 1000, products)),
list(map(lambda p: p.name, products)))
```

Multiplicity of Class Diagram Connections

A relationship between two classes can be depicted as a multiplicity property that an object instantiated from one class is referencing multiple objects instantiated from the other class. This multiplicity property can be represented by a notation drawn next to the arrows, as shown in Figure 5-5a. It is frequently the case that you do not display the class performing the data storage, as shown in Figure 5-5b. This meaning of the two figures is the same, but the second one is most common.

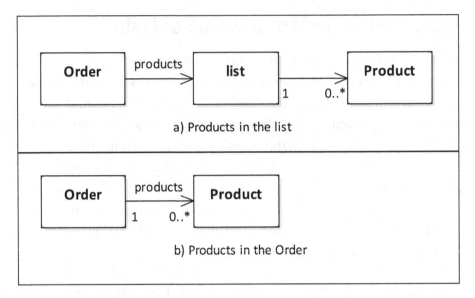

Figures 5-5a and 5-5b. *Relation between products and orders*

Sequence Diagram

The sequence diagram can depict how objects are communicating with each other. A so-called lifeline on the diagram—denoting typically an executing function object or an object that has methods that are called—is denoted by rectangles with a vertical line under them. The horizontal lines with arrowheads show the communication between the lifelines. The timing of the communication is represented by the vertical order of the arrows as the first call is the topmost one and the last one is the bottommost one. The vertical lines show that the objects are available, and their parts can be thickened to show they are actively executed.

Key Takeaways

- Lists are the simplest and most frequently used data structures, which stores objects with before/after relationships. Objects in the lists are referenced by their index number.

- Dictionaries are probably the second most important data structure, in which you map key objects to value objects. Objects in the dictionary can be referenced by keys. Sets can be considered a special case of dictionaries with no value objects assigned to them; only the presence or absence of the keys can be queried.

- Iterable objects can return a sequence of elements one by one and signal if there are no more elements. An object with this kind of property is expected by the for statement. The data structures described in this chapter can behave as iterable classes, and their instances can return sequences of the stored objects in some order (in the case of lists, this happens according to the index numbers of the objects, while in the case of dictionaries it happens in the addition order of the objects).

## CHAPTER 6

The Module: Organization of Program Parts into a Unit

... reuse components that are already available, compose applications from big chunks of premade libraries, glue them together, and make sure it works, even without fully understanding how. Although many would reject this point of view, it is the de facto style, mostly unconsciously, behind today's biggest software projects.

Jaroslav Tulach

When developing computer programs, perhaps the most important question is how to organize your program into logical units. Two of the three most important constructions supporting this goal, namely, functions and classes, have already been discussed. What has not been discussed yet is the next organizational unit above the class, the *module*. The related variable names, functions, and classes are usually organized

© Gabor Guta 2022
G. Guta, *Pragmatic Python Programming*, https://doi.org/10.1007/978-1-4842-8152-9_6

into a module. In this chapter, we will discuss the concepts of modules and packages, how they can be imported, the built-in and third-party packages, how packages can be created, and what kind of tools can help to make packages high quality.

Built-in Modules

Python comes with more than 200 built-in modules, including everything from specialized data structures to relational database management functionality. This is also the reason behind one of the slogans of Python, namely, "batteries included."

You reference a module by using the import keyword and specifying the name of the module. The module containing the date type is imported on line 1 of Listing 6-1 and used on line 2. Modules are also objects, so, for example, classes defined in them can be accessed by putting a dot between the module name and the class name.

Listing 6-1. Importing a Module

```
import datetime
datetime.date(2020,2,2).strftime('%Y.%m.%d.')
```

When a module is frequently used and its name is lengthy, a shorter name can be defined after the as keyword. As shown in Listing 6-2, the example module name is shortened to dt.

Listing 6-2. Importing a Module with a New Name

```
import datetime as dt
dt.date(2020,2,2).strftime('%Y.%m.%d.')
```

Variable names, functions, and classes can be imported selectively from a module. It is also possible in this case to assign another name to the imported object, as shown in Listing 6-3 and Listing 6-4.

Listing 6-3. Importing an Object from a Module

```
from datetime import date
date(2020,2,2).strftime('%Y.%m.%d.')
```

Listing 6-4. Importing an Object from a Module with a New Name

```
from datetime import date as Date
Date(2020,2,2).strftime('%Y.%m.%d.')
```

During the import, even multiple names of classes, functions, or variable names can be specified after the from keyword in a list. The difference between dates is a time difference object. Listing 6-5 shows how to test whether the difference of two dates is more than 30 days.

Listing 6-5. Operations with Date Type

```
from datetime import date, timedelta
date(2020,2,2)-date(2020,1,1) > timedelta(days=30)
```

The float type used so far is not suitable to store financial data, as it performs rounding of the decimal places based on standards usual in mathematics. This is the reason why only an integer type is used for this purpose so far. Therefore, to store financial data, the decimal package is recommended. This package defines the decimal type that can be used, as shown in Listing 6-6. Decimal numbers are specified generally as strings, and the value of the decimal object will match exactly with the number described by the string. Listing 6-7 compares the float type and decimal type. The first value will be a number, which approximates 1.10000000000000088, while the second one will be exactly 1.1.

Listing 6-6. Importing Decimal Types

```
from decimal import Decimal
VALUE_DEC = Decimal('9.45')
```

Listing 6-7. Comparing the Precision of Number Types

```
FLOAT_NUM = 1.1
FINANCIAL_NUM = Decimal('1.1')
print(f'{FLOAT_NUM:.50f}, {FINANCIAL_NUM:.50f},')
```

The result of an operation between two decimals (i.e. how the result is rounded and the number of its stored digits) depends on the environment of the calculation. In Listing 6-8, the environment of the calculation is accessed by the getcontext() function. The listing shows how to use the two instance variables from among the numerous settings: the prec variable specifies the number of stored digits (before and after the decimal point together), and the rounding variable controls the rounding rules (to apply the rules used in standard rounding or in banker's rounding, the ROUND_HALF_UP or ROUND_HALF_EVEN value has to be set, respectively). These settings affect operations only on decimal numbers. During the operations it can happen that the decimal digits produced by the calculation exceed the precision of the original numbers. This can be restored to the accuracy specified in the parameter by the quantize() method.

Listing 6-8. Operations with Decimal Type

```
from decimal import getcontext, ROUND_HALF_UP
getcontext().rounding = ROUND_HALF_UP
getcontext().prec=28
PRICE=Decimal('33')
VAT=Decimal('1.1')
total=(PRICE*VAT).quantize(Decimal('0.01'))
print(f'{total:.20f}')
```

The other important module—containing various extra data structures—is a collection. The deque type—a double-ended queue—is imported in Listing 6-9. This is a list type optimized to be manipulated from both sides (beginning and end) by adding new elements or removing elements. In line 1 of Listing 6-10, a deque with four elements is assigned to the variable name index_numbers. A new element is appended to this list in line 2 in the usual way. Then the first element, whose value is 1 in this example, from the beginning of the index_numbers is removed in the last line.

Listing 6-9. Importing the Deque Type

```
from collections import deque
```

Listing 6-10. Operations with the Deque Type

```
index_numbers = deque((1, 2, 3, 4))
index_numbers.append(5)

index_numbers.popleft()
```

Python searches for the module to be imported first among the built-in modules. If it cannot be found here, try to load it from the location listed in the path variable of the sys module. (Its value can be checked by printing the value of the path variable name after executing the from sys import path statement.) These are as follows: the current directory (i.e., the directory from which your Python program is started); the directories in the environmental variable PYTHONPATH, which was set by the operating system; and the directories specified during the installation.

Defining Modules

It is simple to prepare your own module in Python as the file containing the source code is considered a module by default. Importing a module in Python means that the source code of that module is executed. To turn a stand-alone Python script into a reusable module, you must make its functionalities accessible through functions or classes. Additionally, the statements that are not intended to be executed when the file is used as a module must be guarded by an if statement. The conditional expression of this if statement is typically __name__=='__main__'. The exact meaning of this if statement is as follows: if the file is imported as a module, the name of the module is assigned to the __name__ variable name, while if the file is executed directly as a script, its value is the __main__ string.

The upcoming listings contain only the most relevant fragments of the files from this point. Listing 6-11 references the classes associated with the Order class (in Listings 3-7, 3-13, 3-17, and 3-20) organized into a file named model.py. You can download the complete file of this module. The first line of the fragment is the condition, which is needed to ensure the rest of the code runs only when launched as an independent program.

Listing 6-11. Fragment of the model.py File

```
if __name__=='__main__':
    customer = Customer('X Y',
        'xy@axonmatics.com',
        '1/1234567',
        Address('1011', 'Budapest',
            'Wombat street 1st', 'HUNGARY'))
    products = [
        Order.Item(Product('A', 'cubE', 1), 2),
        Order.Item(Product('B', 'cubF', 3), 5)
    ]
    order = Order(products, customer)
    print(order)
```

Modules can be run from a command line by specifying the filename after the Python command. If your newly generated file is run with the python model.py command, the defined Order type object will appear on the screen.

Note   In this chapter, some of the examples do not consist of source code written in the Python language but commands writable to the operating system command prompt or shell. We covered how to access the command line on a particular operating system at the end of the Introduction chapter.

Commands that need to run Python may be different depending on the operating system and the environment. After installation, under a Windows OS, the py-3.10 command can be used instead of the python command, while under macOS and Linux the python3.10 command has to be issued.

Packages

Packages are modules containing other modules. They can be used to organize the modules into further units. One package is usually one directory with modules with additionally a file named __init__.py in it. This package can also be placed into another package, and this can be repeated arbitrarily. If this package has to be executable directly, a __main__.py file can be placed in the directory that will contain the code to be executed in such a case only.

A model.py file can be created from the class definitions in Listings 3-7, 3-13, 3-17, 3-20, and 6-11. As an example, a package can be built by creating a registry directory and copying the model.py file into this directory. An empty __init__.py file must be created in this directory too, which can be used in the future to add documentation and statements to be executed when loading the package. The model module from this newly constructed package can be imported with the import registry.model statement.

Future Package

The Python language has a statement that can switch on and off new language additions or change their behavior. This statement is the from __future__ import followed by the name of the feature and can be present only at the beginning of the source file. This statement is a different statement than the earlier reviewed import statement. For compatibility reasons, the __future__ package exists and can be used with other forms of import statements, but this is not to be confused with the previous statement.

Since version 3.7, the only active feature that can be turned on is the delayed evaluation of the type annotations, and the name of this feature is *annotations* (see PEP563; type annotations will be discussed in Appendix C). This functionality is turned on by default starting from version 3.11, and in later versions this statement will not change the behavior of the language anymore.

Package Management

The Python environment supports managing third-party packages with a package managing tool named pip. This package manager is able to download versions of the package together with their dependencies from the Python Package Index and make it available to your machine.

Listing 6-12 shows the most important package management commands.

Listing 6-12. Package Management Commands

```
python -m pip list
python -m pip list --outdated
python -m pip search requests
python -m pip install requests
python -m pip install requests ==2.20
python -m pip install requests --upgrade
python -m pip show requests
python -m pip freeze > requirements.txt
python -m pip install -r requirements.txt
```

The first two commands list all the installed packages and all packages having a more up-to-date version than the one installed. The command in line 3 lists packages from the Python Package Index that match the requested word. Lines 4 and 5 show how simple it is to install a package (in the second case, a version number is also specified; a relation sign can also be used here to express the required package version more loosely). The command in line 6 shows information about the installed package, such as the list of packages this one depends on. The last two lines show how to save the list of the installed packages into a file and how to install packages based on a dependency file.

Useful Third-Party Packages

Two scenarios of using third-party packages will be presented in this section. In the first scenario, a web page is downloaded, and information is extracted from the downloaded page. In another scenario, an Excel table is processed.

The package `requests` will download the web page, while the HTML processing will be carried out with the `bs4` package. In the other scenario, the `pandas` package will load an Excel table and answer queries about it. This package can also be connected to databases and import data from other data formats. Listing 6-13 shows how to install the corresponding packages for the two scenarios.

Listing 6-13. Installation of Third-Party Packages

```
python -m pip install requests
python -m pip install beautifulsoup4
python -m pip install pandas
python -m pip install openpyxl
```

Note   The commands needed to install the package may depend on the operating system and the environment. If you have installed the default environment described in the introduction, these commands are as follows: in the case of Windows 10, replace the `python -m pip` part at the beginning of the commands with `py -3.10 -m pip`; in the case of macOS and Linux, replace the `python -m pip` part at the beginning of the commands with `sudo python3.10 -m pip` or `python3.10 -m pip --user`.

The first step of the first scenario is to import the packages as shown in Listing 6-14. The next step is to download the web page, as shown in Listing 6-15, followed by printing the response code of the download request, type of the content, and format of the text coding. Then the downloaded web page is processed. Listing 6-16 and Listing 6-17 show how the header element of the processed web page and the text of the header element can be accessed, respectively.

Listing 6-14. Importing Requests and bs4 Packages

```
import requests
from bs4 import BeautifulSoup
```

Listing 6-15. Downloading a Website

```
APRESS = 'https://apress.github.io'
Q = APRESS + 'pragmatic-python-programming/quotes.html'
r = requests.get(Q, timeout=1)
print(r.status_code, r.headers['content-type'],
      r.encoding)
site = BeautifulSoup(r.text, 'html.parser')
```

Listing 6-16. Header Element of the Web Page

```
site.head.title
```

Listing 6-17. Header Test of the Web Page

```
site.head.title.text
```

Listing 6-18 shows fragments of the data obtained from the website. Listing 6-19 shows the data being processed. This is implemented by iterating through all the tr elements; the class is book, and the text part of the two td elements are printed during this procedure.

Listing 6-18. Fragment of the Web Page

```
<tr class="book">
  <td class="auth">Donald E. Knuth</td>
  <td class="title">TAOCP</td>
</tr>
```

Listing 6-19. Extracting Data from the Body of the Web Page

```
for row in site.find_all('tr',
        class_='book'):
    cells = row.find_all('td')
    print(cells[0].text, ': ',
        cells[1].text, sep='')
```

In the second scenario, the pandas package is imported, and the Excel table is loaded according to Listing 6-20. To display the loaded table, the orders variable is printed.

Listing 6-20. Importing the pandas Package

```
import pandas as pd
orders = pd.read_excel('orders.xlsx',
                        index_col=0)
```

On the loaded tables, different kinds of queries can be executed. The table is sorted according to column 1 in Listing 6-21. In turn, values of the orders are grouped by the customer ID in Listing 6-22.

Listing 6-21. Sorting the Table by Order Value

```
orders.sort_values(by='Order value')
```

Listing 6-22. Grouping the Value of the Orders by Customer ID

```
orders.groupby('Customer id').sum()
```

Modules in Practice

Modules are the highest-level organizational unit in the Python language. For the design of the modules, it is important that the related definitions are located in one module following some organizational principle. It is important for the organizational intent (frequently called the *responsibility* of the module) to be documented as well. In Listing 6-23, the beginning and end fragments of the models.py file are shown. At the beginning the module, the documentation includes short and long descriptions of the module and then presents the use of the module. At the end of the module, there is the idiom-like structure, which runs only when the module is directly launched. This section is usually applied when you want your module to work also as an independent command-line program. This example also contains the version number of the module, assigned to the __version__ variable name.

Listing 6-23. Fragment of the Model Module

```
"""Model of the order management

The domain model of order management system is
modeled by these classes. They can be used
to represent an actual order.

    Example usage:

    product = Product('T1', 'A product', 100)
    product.reduce_price(10)
"""
```

```
__version__ = '1.0.0'
...
if __name__=='__main__':
   ...
```

Modules are frequently written to be reusable, and it's helpful when the functionality of the module can be accessed via a class providing a simplified interaction. This is called a *facade designing pattern*, and it has two benefits: the module does not have to know the exact internal structure of the module, and using the module takes place on a well-specified "narrow" surface. Therefore, in the case of an internal change, other modules using this one would not need to be changed. Developing an easily reusable module can be even three times more effort than developing a module for only a single use.

Advanced Concepts

This section describes some technical details in reference manual style and some advanced concepts that may need more technical background.

Structure of Python Projects

Several recommendations exist for the structure of Python projects, which differ in detail like the format used to store dependencies or the package description (often named README) file. The recommended location of the source files is the src directory. Depending on whether the program contains one or more files, the src directory contains a single Python source file named identically with the package name or a directory named identically to the package name. In addition, it usually includes a tests directory for the tests and a docs directory of the documentation. In addition, the project usually includes a LICENSE file containing a description of the license and/or a package description file. This file is named README.md or README.rst depending on whether markdown or reStructuredText is chosen as a format, respectively. In the simplest case, the dependencies of our module on third-party packages are stored in a requirements.txt file. If you want to share/publish your module, you will also need a setup.py file, pyproject.toml file, or other files that can also substitute the function of requirements.txt as well.

If you want the Python package to be available for others, you can prepare a compressed file from it suitable for binary distribution. This file can be shared manually or can be uploaded to a package index server. This server can be the default pypi.org or any other repository server. Packages can be configured classically with a setup.py file, which stores the package information (such as version, author, dependencies, license, and the like) programmatically. New versions of tools support to substitute the setup.py file with a configuration file, which is named pyproject.toml and contains the necessary information to describe the package.

Listing 6-24 shows the content of the setup.py file. If this file is executed with the python setup.py bdist command, it will generate a compressed package file in the build directory. For example, this file would be named registry-1.0.win-amd64.zip.

Listing 6-24. The setup.py File

```
from setuptools import setup
setup(name='registry',
      version='1.0.0',
      description='Order Management System',
      author='Gabor Guta, PhD',
      author_email='info@axonmatics.com',
      license='GPL',
      packages=['registry'],
      package_dir={'':'src'},
      python_requires='>=3.10')
```

To transition to the new approach, you need the install the build package and update the setuptools package. This can be achieved with the pip install --upgrade setuptools build command. The contents of pyproject.toml and setup.cfg are shown in Listing 6-25 and Listing 6-26, respectively. The command python -m build can be used to generate the registry-1.0.0-py2.py3-none-any.whl and registry-1.0.0.tar.gz compressed package files.

Listing 6-25. The pyproject.toml File

```
[build-system]
requires = ["setuptools"]
build-backend = "setuptools.build_meta"
```

Listing 6-26. The setup.cfg File

```
[metadata]
name = registry
version = 1.0.0
description = Order Management System
author = Gabor Guta, PhD
author_email = info@axonmatics.com
license = GPL

[options]
package_dir =
    = src
packages = find:
python_requires = >=3.10

[options.packages.find]
where=src
```

Virtual Environments

The virtual environment can be useful when the exact reproducibility of the environment is important or you have to use various Python versions and package versions in parallel. The virtual environment can be created by the `python -m venv ENVIRONMENT_NAME` command, where `ENVIRONMENT_NAME` is the name of the environment to be created. The environment will be created in a directory named the same as the name specified in the command. The directory will contain a `pyvenv.cfg` configuration file; an `include` directory for the C header files; a `lib` directory, which contains the `site-packages` directory for the third-party packages; and finally, a `bin` or `Scripts` directory—depending on whether the installation is under Linux or Windows—containing program files of the Python environment. The environment can be activated with the `source ENVIRONMENT_NAME/bin/activate` command on Linux, while the same can be accomplished by the `ENVIRONMENT_NAME\script\activate.bat` command on Windows 10. The environment can be switched off by the `deactivate` command. (The macOS commands are identical to the commands used for Linux.)

Other tools are also available to manage the virtual environments. The most popular alternatives for the built-in tools are the `pipenv` and `poetry` tools.

Tools for Testing

Python provides built-in packages to make testing easier. The most important package is the `unittest` package, which supports the automatic testing of functions and classes. A test case class typically contains test methods, which exercise functionalities and verify that the functionality worked as expected. Often special `setUp` and `tearDown` methods are used to prepare the test method and clean up the environment after the execution of the method, respectively. The verification of the functionality is typically realized by calling assert methods to compare actual results to the expected results. Test cases can be organized into test suites.

Listing 6-27 shows a test class to test the Product class. The first method instantiates a Product object. This method is called each time before the execution of other test methods. The second method is the first actual test: it verifies that the attributes of the tested object are initialized correctly. The third function calls a method of the object and verifies that the price and old_price data attributes have changed as expected. Finally, the last method verifies that the method terminates with an exception in the case of an invalid parameter value.

Listing 6-27. Unit Test of the Product Class

```python
from unittest import TestCase

class TestProduct(TestCase):
    def setUp(self):
        self.prod = Product('K01', 'Standard Cube', 1000)

    def test_product_creation(self):
        self.assertEqual(self.prod.code, 'K01')
        self.assertEqual(self.prod.name, 'Standard Cube')
        self.assertEqual(self.prod.price, 1000)
        self.assertEqual(self.prod.old_price, 1000)

    def test_price_reduction(self):
        self.prod.reduce_price(10)
        self.assertEqual(self.prod.price, 900)
        self.assertEqual(self.prod.old_price, 1000)

    def test_invalid_input(self):
        with self.assertRaises(TypeError):
            self.prod.reduce_price("A")
```

If you are interested in testing, two topics may be worth further study:

- How can functionalities that require complex environments be tested in isolation with the help packages like the `unittest.mock` package?

- What are the popular tools to ease testing like the `pytest` framework?

Tools for Static Analysis

Several tools are available to automatically identify suspected errors in the code. Only two popular tools that can help to ensure the quality of the Python code will be shown in this section. One is `pylint`, which basically checks syntactic patterns and the formatting rules described in PEP8. The other tool is `mypy`, which can perform static type checking based on the type annotations. Listing 6-28 shows how to use them.

Listing 6-28. Static Analysis Commands

```
python -m pip install pylint
python -m pip install mypy
pylint src/registry
mypy --strict src/registry
```

There is an option for both tools to include comments in the source file, which disable some of the checks of the tool. This is useful when you intentionally do not want to comply with the default checking rules for some reason.

Tools for Formatting

Python code formatters are useful to automatically make your source code easier to read and conform to the PEP8 standard. There are several such tools like autopep8 or yapf, but the most popular tool is probably black. While the first two of tools can be widely customized, black is famous for providing good results out of the box and hardly allowing any customization in its formatting style.

In Listing 6-29 you can see the installation of the black package and the reformatting of the model.py file.

Listing 6-29. Installing and Using the black Formatting Tool

```
pip install black
black src/registry/model.py
```

Preparation of Documentation

The program Sphynx can be used to generate documentation for your package. Preparing the documentation consists of two steps: the tool extracts the documentation comments from the Python source files, and then it combines them with the documentation files and creates documentation of your package. Documentation files provide the frame of the documentation of the package, and they can also contain further documentation about the package. As an example, a file containing the user guide will be created. A format called reStructuredText can be used to add formatting to the text in the documentation files. Some formatting notation for example: the text highlighting can be denoted by stars put around the text; or the chapter title can be marked by underlining (a series of equal signs in the next line as long as the title text).

Listing 6-30 shows the commands used to generate the documentation. The command in line installs the tool. The documentation files have to be created next, which can be done with the commands in lines 2 and 3. After executing the sphinx-quickstart command, select the no option to answer the source and destination question, name the project registry, set any name for the author's name, and confirm the default option to the last two questions. The default documentation and configuration files are automatically generated by these two commands.

Listing 6-30. Commands to Execute Sphinx

```
python -m pip install sphinx
sphinx-quickstart
sphinx-apidoc -o docs src/registry
make html
```

Thereafter, you can add the user guide shown in Listing 6-31 to your project, by copying the content of the listing into the userguide.rst file in the docs directory. The files that are generated by default require the following modifications: references to the documentation files have to be added in the index.rst file, as shown in Listing 6-32; in the conf.py file, the hash marks before the first three lines have to be removed, the source directory path have to be fixed, and lines 7–10 (the section beginning with the extensions word) should be rewritten as shown in Listing 6-33. These modifications are necessary for Sphynx to be able to automatically load the comments (docstrings) from the Python source files. The command in line 4 will generate the description of the module in HTML format. If the files are changed, the documentation can be regenerated with the last two commands.

Listing 6-31. The File which Contains the Module Description

```
User Guide
=====================

This is the description of the *modul*.
```

Listing 6-32. The Sphinx index.rst File

```
.. toctree::
   :maxdepth: 2
   :caption: Contents:

   docs/userguide
   docs/modules
```

Listing 6-33. The Sphinx conf.py File

```
import os
import sys
sys.path.insert(0, os.path.abspath('./src/'))

# Please, leave the original conent between these two sections

extensions = [
'sphinx.ext.autodoc',
'sphinx.ext.napoleon',
]
```

Key Takeaways

- Functions, classes, and other definitions can be organized into modules to make it easier to navigate between them. A Python source file itself is a module already. A package is a module that contains further modules in it. Modules must be imported before they can be used.

- Packages are usually stored as files. If a package is not included in the built-in Python library, the package file must be copied into your work environment somehow. This problem can be solved with the package manager called pip, which can download and copy the packages into your work environment. The third-party packages used by your program are called the *dependencies* of your program, and it is recommended to list them in a file (e.g., requirements.txt).

- When you're developing a Python program, you have a huge collection of built-in packages that can help you. If this isn't enough, a huge collection of third-party packages are provided by the Python ecosystem.

APPENDIX A

Binary Representation

This appendix discusses how 0s and 1s can be understood by the computer to represent the simple or complicated types shown in the book. For a computer, the 0s and 1s—called *bits*—are organized into groups of eight. This is called a *byte*, which can take 256 different values: 00000000, 00000001, 00000010, 00000011, ..., 11111111.

After refreshing our knowledge on the concept of numeral systems, these bits can be treated as digits in the binary system, behaving similarly to their counterparts in the decimal system. The two main differences are that the highest digit here is the 1 and that the place values of the digits are 1, 2, 4, 8, 16, etc., instead of 1, 10, 100, 1000, etc. That is, 101 is a binary number corresponds to 5 since there is a 1 in the place values of 1 and 4. You can see in Listing A-1 how to display the decimal number 42 as a binary number and how to specify integers as binary numbers.

Listing A-1. Bits

```
print(bin(42))
print(0b101010, int('101010', 2))
```

Several operations can be performed with the numbers in the binary system, which may be hard to understand from the result that appears in the decimal system. Listing A-2 shows how negation (0s are exchanged with 1s, 1s with 0s) and shift operations work. Listing A-3 shows how different bitwise operators work: for the AND, the result is 1 only when both are 1; for OR, the result is 1 if either number is 1; and for the exclusive

© Gabor Guta 2022
G. Guta, *Pragmatic Python Programming*, https://doi.org/10.1007/978-1-4842-8152-9

OR, it is 1 when only one of the numbers is equal to 1. The AND operator is usually applied for masking: those place values that we would like to keep will be given the 1 value, and those to be deleted will be given a 0. In our example, we want to keep only the lowest four place values.

Listing A-2. Simple Operation with Bits

```
print('A:', bin(42), '~:', bin(~42%256),
    '<<:', bin(42<<1), '>>:', bin(42>>1), )
```

Listing A-3. Further Operation with Bits

```
print('A:', bin(42), 'B:', bin(15),
    '&:', bin(42&15),'|:',  bin(42|15),
    '^:',  bin(42^15))
```

Bytes can be stored similarly to strings, except here there is a letter b in front of the quotation marks. Operators are identical to those usual for strings. The bytes type has a modifiable counterpart, the bytearray, that works like a list with the restriction that its elements can be only bytes, as shown in Listing A-4. Objects having bytes and bytearray for the type can be mixed in operators.

Listing A-4. Types to Store Bytes

```
DATA = b'temp'
data_rw = bytearray()
data_rw.extend(DATA)
data_rw.append(5)
print(DATA, data_rw)
```

It was already explained how numbers are represented. Let's look now at characters. Characters are stored such that each letter has a number assigned to it. The code for the letter *t* is 116, as shown in Listing A-5. The code of a character can be queried by the ord() built-in function, while the character belonging to the particular code can be queried by the chr() function.

Listing A-5. Characters as Numbers

```
print(ord('t'), chr(116))
```

Strings and bytes form independent data types since different standards assign different characters to numbers; it is possible even for a character to need multiple bytes to denote it. The standards of code assignments are the so-called code tables, and the most widespread ones currently are the ASCII and UTF-8 tables. The ASCII code assigns characters to a number between 0 and 127, which requires only one byte to store. This is enough to denote letters of the English alphabet, digits, and most important special characters. Table A-1 the codes of the most important characters (these codes are identical in the ASCII and UTF-8 standards). The UTF-8 standard contains a code mapping practically for all characters in the word, because it allows codes to be stored in several bytes. Python uses UTF-8 for storing the strings, while the notation of the bytes allows only the use of ASCII characters.

Listing A-6. Strings and Bytes

```
print(b'temp'.decode())
print('temp ÁÉÍÓÚ'.encode())
```

Table A-1. *ASCII Codes of Some Important Characters*

ASCII Code	Character	ASCII Code	Character
9	\t (TAB)	64	@
10	\n (LF)	65	A
13	\r (CR)	90	Z
32	SPACE	91	[
34	"	92	\
40	(	93	]
41	)	97	a
43	+	122	z
47	/	123	{
48	0	124		
57	9	125	}

It is important to note that the bytes are not intended to represent characters, but only their binary representation. This means that strings that store characters can be converted to bytes according to any code pages. Naturally, not all characters can be represented in all code pages. Listing A-6 shows that a string is created from the bytes from the decode() method and bytes from the strings by the encode() method. In both directions you use the UTF-8 code page. As shown, multiple bytes belong to the accentuated letters.

When representing the integers, you saw how a number in the decimal system is presented in one byte; but what happens when the number is greater than 255? In this case, more than one byte can be used for the representation like two bytes would be connected: one contains the lower place value, while the other one accommodates the higher place value. It is a question of convention whether the lower is written first or the higher one. The former solution is called *little endian* (the lower one goes first) and the latter one *big endian* (the higher one goes first) encoding, as shown in Listing A-7. (If the two encoding systems are exchanged and the values of the two bytes are not identical, the result obtained will be incorrect.) The currently used machines with x86 processors use the little endian encoding, while the network standards use the big endian encoding.

Listing A-7. Representing Integers on Multiple Bytes

```
INTEGER = 768
byte_repr = INTEGER.to_bytes(2, byteorder='little')
reverse = int.from_bytes(byte_repr, byteorder='little')
print(byte_repr, reverse)
```

Floating-point numbers are stored as two integers to encode separately the mantissa and the base. Python stores the floating-point numbers according to the IEEE 754 standard, which describes in detail how these two integers are stored exactly.

Listing A-8 shows the struct package. This package is able to transform most data types to a byte series and vice versa. The conversion to the bytes can be carried out with the pack() function, while converting bytes to other types can be carried out with the unpack() function. For the transformation back and forth, the program expects a format specification string in which the type of the data to be transformed to/from bytes can be specified by a notation.

Listing A-8. Converting Simple Types to Bytes and Back

```
from struct import pack, unpack
print(pack('B', (42)),
      pack('>H', (42)), pack('<H', (42)))
print(unpack('>H', b'\x00*'),
      unpack('<H', b'\x00*')) #42*256
```

APPENDIX B

Type Annotations

Type annotations are currently only for documentation purposes. The Python language does not use this information in any form. These annotations are usually applied for two reasons: static type checking programs are able to verify whether the particular variable name will make reference only to the denoted type of objects without running the program; and the integrated development environments (IDEs) can provide better type hinting and code completion.

Annotations of the most important built-in types were shown in the first three chapters. For the more complex type annotations, you need to import the typing module. This module contains definitions of the data structure and the various type modifiers. More complex type annotations are shown in Listing B-1.

- a: A list of integers (the types of the list elements are in square brackets)

- b: A set of strings (the types of the set elements are in square brackets)

- c: A dictionary with string keys and float values (the types of dictionary keys and values are in square brackets)

- d: A pair, the first element of which is a string, and its second element is an integer (the types of the elements by position are in square brackets)

© Gabor Guta 2022

G. Guta, *Pragmatic Python Programming*, https://doi.org/10.1007/978-1-4842-8152-9

- e: An integer or None (Optional means the None value is also allowed)

- f: An integer or string (the union indicates that both types are allowed)

- g: Any type

Listing B-1. Type Annotations

```
from typing import (Optional, Union, Any)
a: list[int] = [1, 2, 4, 8]
b: set[str] = {'a', 'b', 'c'}
c: dict[str, float] = {'a': 2.3, 'b': 5.5}
d: tuple[str, int] = ('a', 1)
e: Optional[int] = None
e = 3
f: Union[int, str] = 3
f = 'hello'
g: Any = 3
g = 'hello'
```

An alias can be generated for types to avoid having to repeat a complicated type expression. A tuple is visible in Listing B-2, the first two elements of which are strings and the last is a number. Values stored in identical types but having different meanings are interchangeable by mistake. This can be prevented by introducing a new type. The first two strings in this example (though the first one is a product ID and the second one is a product name) are error prone with the default type annotation. Listing B-3 demonstrates how this source of mistake can be prevented by introducing new types: ProductId and ProductName are defined as subtypes of the string. This type annotation makes possible static verification of the usage of correct types.

Listing B-2. Type Alias

```
ProductRecord = Tuple[str, str, int]
```

Listing B-3. New Type Definition

```
from typing import NewType
ProductId = NewType('ProductId', str)
ProductName = NewType('ProductName', str)
TypedProductRecord = Tuple[ProductId, ProductName, int]
```

As mentioned previously, in the Python language typing can be based on protocols. If a class has the expected methods, it can be regarded to be a specific type. For the annotation of this, the Protocol type can be used. Listing B-4 shows that by specifying whether a class has a reduce_price() method or not, it will be regarded as a Discountable type.

Listing B-4. Protocol Type

```
from typing import Protocol
class Discountable(Protocol):
    def reduce_price(self, percent: int) -> int:
        ...
```

The generic types are suitable for defining a function or a class in a way types of certain parameters or returning values could be specified later. In the case of a generic type definition, it is specified only which ones have to be identical from among the types to be specified later or whether some kind of restriction applies to the deferred type definitions. In Listing B-5, types of the price and of the function calculating the reduced price should be the same and suitable to store the financial value. This is attained in the example by allowing only the specification of int or Decimal types.

Listing B-5. Generic Type

```
from decimal import Decimal
from typing import TypeVar, Callable

#Number suitable for a financial operation
FN = TypeVar('FN', int, Decimal)

def discounted_value(price: FN, amount: int,
    sale: Callable[[FN, int], FN]) -> FN:
    value: FN = price * amount
    discount: FN = sale(price, amount)
    return value*(1-discount)

print('Result of the example call of discount_value function:',
    discount_value(1000, 10, lambda p, q: 0.1 if p*q >
    5000 else 0))
```

APPENDIX C

Asynchronous Programming

In general, *asynchronous* behavior means that we do not wait for the effect of a triggered event. As an example, after sending a message, the sender will not wait for the response but will continue to the next step, and the response will be handled when it arrives. This makes sense because it's the opposite of the usual *synchronous* behavior when the process blocks until the arrival of the response.

Executing slow parts of a program (functions reading data from a hard disk or from the network) asynchronously makes it possible to execute further program parts until the requested data arrives. To implement this, Python provides various language constructs and the `asyncio` package. Additionally, several third-party packages support asynchronous functionality such as `aiofile`, `aiohttp`, `asyncpg`, etc. In this appendix, the goal is to explain the behavior of the language constructs connected to the native coroutines and the necessary parts of the `asyncio` package.

© Gabor Guta 2022
G. Guta, *Pragmatic Python Programming*, https://doi.org/10.1007/978-1-4842-8152-9

Note   It is important to clarify the concepts of concurrent and parallel execution as they are often referenced in a confusing manner. Let's start with *parallel execution*: this means that parts of the program are executed on two or more physical computational units (cores, processors, or machines).

Concurrent execution means that parts of the programs run in an interleaving way; i.e., one part of the program does not wait for the completion of the other parts before it starts. Naturally, these parts can be executed in parallel, but often concurrency is realized in a way that program parts execute in chunks. The execution of the parts is coordinated partly by the environment, but the program parts usually have to support this by a cooperative behavior of signaling when they can pass the control to another part.

You can achieve asynchronous behavior with native coroutines, which are defined as the functions or methods prefixed with an extra `async` keyword. These coroutines can create coroutine objects when they are called, which can be awaited. The execution of awaitable objects is supported by the `asyncio` package. This package contains various low-level and high-level functions, but as mentioned earlier, this appendix will just explain the bare minimum of the high-level functionality.

The Python language has two different kinds of coroutines: the generator-based coroutine already discussed in Chapter 5 and the native coroutine. Although their names sound similar, they work fairly differently. So, the native coroutine will be introduced as a new building block of the language. From now on, by *coroutine*, I mean *native coroutine function* if it is not specified explicitly otherwise.

Listing C-1 shows how a coroutine called main can be executed. Note that if main is simply called with a function call operator like main(), it won't execute; it will just return a coroutine object. In Figure C-1, the process of executing the main coroutine can be traced: when the coroutine is called, it returns a coroutine object, which is passed to the asyncio.run function for execution. This function internally wraps the coroutine object into a Task and runs it on the so-called event loop. The event loop is responsible for switching to the next executable Task if there are any.

Listing C-1. A Native Coroutine

```
import asyncio

async def main():
    print('Hello World!')

asyncio.run(main())
```

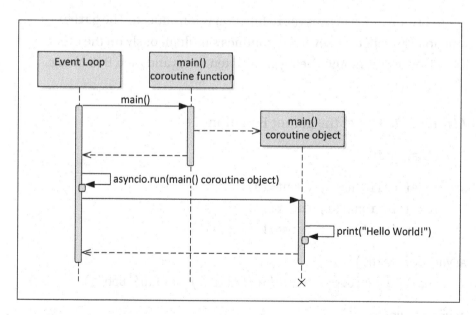

Figure C-1. *A native coroutine execution*

183

Listing C-2 shows that a coroutine has to use the `await` statement to execute another coroutine. The `await` statement can be used only inside a coroutine and expects an awaitable object. This listing practically chains two coroutines. The `hello` coroutine prints the greeting with the specified name 10 times if it is not parameterized differently.

Listing C-2. Usage of the await Statement

```
import asyncio

async def hello(name, count=10):
    for i in range(1, count+1):
        print(f'Hello {name}! (x {i})')

async def main():
    await hello("World", 1)

asyncio.run(main())
```

In Listing C-3, a new `asyncio` function is introduced. The `gather` function can schedule several coroutines simultaneously on the event loop. This results in Alice being greeted ten times and then Bob being greeted ten times.

Listing C-3. Use of the gather Function

```
import asyncio

async def hello(name, count=10):
    for i in range(1, count+1):
        print(f'Hello {name}! (x {i})')

async def main():
    await asyncio.gather(hello("Alice"), hello("Bob"))

asyncio.run(main())
```

Listing C-4 shows that the hello coroutine is slightly changed by adding 0 seconds of delay after printing the greeting. When calling the sleep function, you can signal to the event loop that other tasks can be scheduled. This results in the interleaving printing of the greeting for Alice and Bob. Figure C-2 shows three steps of this interleaving behavior.

Listing C-4. Usage of the sleep Function

```python
import asyncio

async def hello(name, count=10, delay=0):
    for i in range(1, count+1):
        print(f'Hello {name}! (x {i})')
        await asyncio.sleep(delay)

async def main():
    await asyncio.gather(hello("Alice"), hello("Bob"))

asyncio.run(main())
```

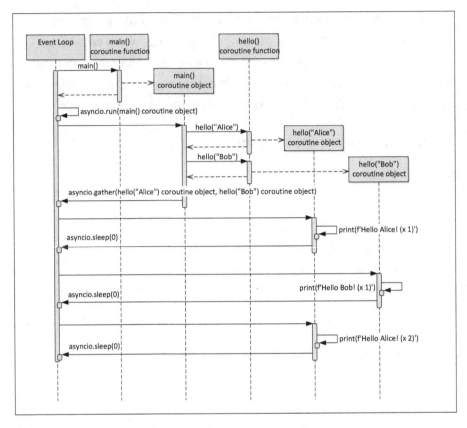

Figure C-2. *Execution of multiple native coroutines*

In Listing C-5 the explicit creation of Tasks can be seen. Tasks can be imagined as handlers that store the execution states of the coroutines. In this example, two coroutines are executed one after each other. The variable names task_a and task_b reference the corresponding tasks, and the print(task_a.done(), task_b.done()) calls print the status of the two tasks. The statement await task_b will wait until the hello coroutine, which greets Bob five times, finishes. It is expected that by reaching the last status message both tasks are completed.

Listing C-5. Use of the create_task Function

```python
import asyncio

async def hello(name, count=10, delay=0):
    for i in range(1, count+1):
        print(f'Hello {name}! (x {i})')
        await asyncio.sleep(delay)

async def main():
    task_a = asyncio.create_task(hello("Alice", count=10,
    delay=1))
    task_b = asyncio.create_task(hello("Bob", count=5,
    delay=1))
    print(task_a.done(), task_b.done())
    await task_b # approx. 5 sec
    print(task_a.done(), task_b.done())
    await asyncio.sleep(10) # approx. 2+4 sec
    print(task_a.done(), task_b.done())

asyncio.run(main())
```

In Listing C-6 an asynchronous generator can be seen. It is defined similarly to a coroutine but contains at least one yield statement. It can return an asynchronous iterator calling the aiter function on its instance. The asynchronous iterator returns awaitable objects and can be queried with the anext() function. Asynchronous iterators can be consumed by async for statements, as shown in the listing.

187

Listing C-6. An Asynchronous Generator

```python
import asyncio

async def hello(name, count, delay=0):
    for i in range(1, count+1):
        print(f'Hello {name}! (x {i})')
        await asyncio.sleep(delay)

async def hello_gen(name, count, delay=0):
    for i in range(1, count+1):
        print('Returned a value {count} (x {i})')
        yield f'Hello {name}! (x {i})'
        await asyncio.sleep(delay)

async def main():
    task_a = asyncio.create_task(hello("Alice", 10, delay=1))
    async for message_b in hello_gen("Bob", 10, delay=1):
        print(message_b)
    await task_a

asyncio.run(main())
```

There is an `async with` statement that expects an asynchronous context manager; otherwise, it works similarly to a `with` statement. All statements starting with the `async` keyword can be used only in the coroutines or asynchronous generators.

Bibliography

1. Kent Beck, Ward Cunningham. A laboratory for teaching object oriented thinking. *Proceedings of OOPSLA '89*, Pages 1-6, ACM, 1989

2. Michael R. Blaha, James R. Rumbaugh. *Object-Oriented Modeling and Design with UML* (2nd edition). Pearson, 2004

3. Robert L. Glass. *Facts and Fallacies of Software Engineering*. Addison-Wesley Professional, 2002

4. Brian W. Kernighan, Dennis M. Ritchie. *The C programming language* (2nd ed.). Prentice Hall, 1988

5. Russ Miles, Kim Hamilton. *Learning UML 2.0*. O'Reilly Media, 2006

6. Donald E. Knuth. *The Art of Computer Programming, Vol. 1: Fundamental Algorithms* (3rd ed.). Addison Wesley Professional, 1997

7. John McCarthy. *LISP I programmer's manual*. Massachusetts Institute of Technology, Computation Center and Research Laboratory of Electronics, 1960

8. Guido van Rossum. Language Design Is Not Just Solving Puzzles. `https://www.artima.com/weblogs/viewpost.jsp?thread=147358`, 2006

9. Jaroslav Tulach. Practical API Design: *Confessions of a Java Framework Architect.* Apress, 2008.

10. David West. *Object Thinking.* Microsoft Press, 2004

11. Beautiful Soup 4.4.0 documentation. `https://www.crummy.com/software/BeautifulSoup/bs4/doc/`, 2022

12. Black documentation. `https://black.readthedocs.io/en/stable/`, 2022

13. Pandas User Guide. `https://pandas.pydata.org/pandas-docs/stable/user_guide/index.html`, 2022

14. Pipenv: Python Dev Workflow for Humans. `https://pipenv.pypa.io/en/latest/`, 2022

15. + Poetry – Documentation. `https://python-poetry.org/docs/`, 2022

16. Pylint User Manual. `http://pylint.pycqa.org/en/latest/`, 2022

17. PyPI: The Python Package Index. `http://pypi.org`, 2022

18. Pytest. `https://docs.pytest.org/en/7.1.x/`, 2022

19. Python 3.10.2 documentation. `https://docs.python.org/3/`, 2022

20. Requests: HTTP for Humans. `https://requests.readthedocs.io/en/master/`, 2022

21. Setuptools – Documentation. `https://setuptools.pypa.io/en/latest/`, 2022

22. Sphinx documentation. `https://www.sphinx-doc.org/en/master/`, 2020

23. Mypy documentation. `https://mypy.readthedocs.io/en/stable/`, 2022

Index

A

Absolute value, 26

Abstract base classes (ABC classes), 72, 73

Accessing an object, 116

Activity diagram, 113

all() function, 125

Annotations, 177, 179

Arguments, 26, 29

ASCII code, 173

Assert statement, 37

Assignment expression, 93

Asynchronous behavior, 142, 181, 182

Asynchronous functionality, 181

Asynchronous generator, 187, 188

Asynchronous iterators, 187

asyncio package, 181, 182

Attributes, 48, 68, 78

Await statement, 184

B

BaseException class, 111

Big endian, 175

Binary representation, 174–178

Bits, 171, 172

Blocks, 1, 23, 25, 31

Boolean expression, 4, 37, 81, 82, 84, 86

Boolean type object, 66

Boolean types, 3–5

break statement, 96

Bytes, 172–175

C

Characters, special meaning, 21

Class

    ABC, 72, 73

    data classes, 73–75

    defining, 51, 52, 154

    diagrams, 77

    identification methods, 76

    immutable objects, 73–75

    inheritance, 61–63

    instance variables, 49

    instantiation, 53–55

    nested classes, 64, 65

    objects, 49

    in practice, 68, 69

    relationships, 55–58

    responsibilities, 49

    special methods, 65–67

    variables, 70

© Gabor Guta 2022
G. Guta, *Pragmatic Python Programming*, https://doi.org/10.1007/978-1-4842-8152-9